Leader Spider Print Co.

The Key to the Kingdom

Heaven upon earth

Leader Spider Print Co.

The Key to the Kingdom
Heaven upon earth

ISBN/EAN: 9783337247850

Printed in Europe, USA, Canada, Australia, Japan

Cover: Foto ©Lupo / pixelio.de

More available books at **www.hansebooks.com**

THE
Key to the Kingdom,
OR
Heaven upon Earth.

SAN FRANCISCO:
LEADER PRINTING CO., 532 COMMERCIAL STREET.
1891.

TO MY CHILDREN.

This little work is dedicated to my four dear children who have unremittingly sustained me for years, by their diligence and happy hearts. The appellation, "spider" which they gave me endeared itself to me, and I thought to partially repay them, I would weave or spin a silvery web that it might unite us more closely to him we love, and who is our sustainer in truth, for in him "we live, and move, and have our being." He gives all things freely for the asking.

Mama.

PSALM LXII.

Truly my soul waiteth upon God from him cometh my salvation.

He only is my rock and my salvation; he is my defence; I shall not be greatly moved.

How long will ye imagine mischief against a man? Ye shall be slain all of you: as a bowing wall shall ye be, and as a tottering fence.

They only consult to cast him down from his excellency: they delight in lies: they bless with their mouth, but they curse inwardly.

My soul, wait thou only upon God; for my expectation is from him.

He only is my rock and my salvation: he is my defence; I shall not be moved.

In God is my salvation and my glory: the rock of my strength, and my refuge, is in God.

Trust in him at all times; ye people, pour out your heart before him; God is a refuge for us.

Surely men of low degree are vanity, and men of high degree are a lie: to be laid in the balance, they are altogether lighter than vanity.

Trust not in oppression, and become not vain in robbery: if riches increase, set not your heart upon them.

PREFACE.

The spider taketh hold with her hands and is in kings' palaces. —Prov. xxx: 28.

Dilligence hath its reward. We write this epistle to those who are weary of creeds and dogmas, and who have not yet found the kingdom of heaven within. Our weapon of defense is knowledge. We could not write unless we had the standard. We do not tear down, for in the inner meaning of His Word we find all things are necessary to operate upon the mind in its feebleness. As wisdom opens the door into the kingdom called heaven, we ask you to seek, if you would find the key. The work of reformation or regeneration must be actualized in the individual soul, then we cross the Jordan and enter the land flowing with milk and honey. It is a truth, not as we read of in Rev. T. DeWitt Talmage's book. He reads to his party of Christ's baptism in the Jordan, and goes into the river with a candidate to immerse his body. He tells us this symbol has been used in all ages to divide heaven from earth. The doctor goes on to say he reported to no particular denomination of Christians (quite liberal). We go further, for we know it is not the dipping of ones body into a river that converts the mind from a state of ignorance to one of enlightenment. We know that water in all its forms is expressive of creative power, and we also know that the symbol as used by Dr. Talmage or any other person must in time wear itself out, for the law holds good; the shadow must pass away. "The heavens declare the glory of God, and the firmament showeth his handiwork: day unto day uttereth speech, and night unto night showeth knowledge." All things speak to us when we can reason, and think, compare and form similitudes. It is the meaning of Adam. We are to stand firm on our feet, with God to guide us.

The commercial world has its rules and measurements to guide and govern the mind, that all who adhere to them may work in harmony. The time is at hand that the least shall be greatest. The spiritual has not as yet set and fixed rules firmly established, nor can it have until the cry goes forth for equity and justice. Then comes the awakening, for the soul is crushed, and cries out as did Saul, "What wilt thou have me do?"

The law through Moses came, then the prophets were sent to us, but now we want the truth, the whole truth, and nothing but the truth, which gives us the standard, the true rock of reason. It is then we are blest by the new dispensation, for the truth sets all free, every tribe, tongue and nation.

> The gods of our fathers we cannot adore;
> It's the River of Water, of Life we explore.
> And our minds then unfold according to law;
> We leave all in kindness, but truth we adore.

We admire Japhet, but love Shem, and we know in time that Japhet will come into the tents of Shem to dwell. God hears our prayer, and we send the "Key" to open the door that all may enter the eternal kingdom and be forever and ever blest. If we are faithful over a few things, He will make us ruler over many, and our joy will be complete. Thus the spider, as the smallest, gets into the highest place—the palace, and weaves a web to catch the wise ones.

Remember the little child state, and be ye not puffed up with vain glory.

Heaven is that which is wrought, established. Begin now to reconstruct. The soul is the center, and as your mind unfolds, the light will shine for you as it did for Paul, but like Paul you may not be on the right path, although joined to the straightest sect or religion. Adieu, we leave you with the "Key."

The Key to the Kingdom

OR

Heaven upon Earth.

This planet as a seed or soul was sent forth by His word and represents Elohim as motion, which caused the nebulous mass to become detached, and to revolve around some previously created center. It took ages to bring about a state of perfection in the order of planets, still unproductive of life.

Then, as the planet became sufficiently cooled and encrusted, the power of God again went forth, and each order and kingdom were successively established, the mineral, vegetable and animal.

The animal most nearly resembling the human was selected as our forerunner, and the soul of man was sent from the realms of perfection to begin the work of regeneration. It has been going on since Adam, and yet we are not able to read "our title clear to mansions in the skies." We should be willing to hear all things pertaining to our creation and perfection. We must in time be perfect, as God is perfection. There is within us an innate desire to know God because we emanated from the deity.

The human body as a microcosm or little world is an image of the macrocosm or great world. Whatever principles of science have been discovered in mechanics, chemistry, hydraulics, hydrostatics, botany, electricity, etc., are perfectly portrayed in the functions and uses of the human frame.

Thus the body is the temple of sciences, both physical and philosophical.

Pray ye that your flight be not in the winter when a cold-hearted selfishness has taken possession of mind. Matt. 20: 5.

As the people of Israel had to pass through the desert before they could arrive at the land flowing with milk and honey, so we, as their representatives, have had to pass through all the signs and forms, parables and allegories, that have been given to us from time to time, to prepare our minds that we might in time gain the promised land.

Israel means one who prevails with heaven; and heaven is a state of consciousness reached through the mind if a cold-hearted selfishness has not taken possession of us.

Then Israel leads us to the land flowing with milk and honey, which types food for the soul.

On the other hand "The harvest is passed, and the summer is ended, and we are not saved." Jer. 8: 20.

What does salvation consist of? This is our work. We desire to prove God's wisdom in all things; and to make clear to those who are brokenhearted the way unto salvation.

God said in the beginning, "Let there be light." It was a prophetical fiat. The light of the Logos or Word is here awaiting recognition, but who is prepared to receive it?

Let us dispossess our minds of the cold-hearted selfishness that has taken possession of us, and acknowledge the dreary march through the desert; turn not to man; seek God, for the light or reason will guide you safely through, follow Him who calls Himself "Lord of the harvest," and who tells us that we may reap life everlasting if we will follow Him.

Then if any man shall say unto you "Lo! here is Christ, or there; believe it not. For there shall arise false Christs and false prophets, and shall show great signs and wonders, insomuch that, if it were possible, they shall deceive the very elect."

We have been granted a pleasure in finding what perhaps you have not found—the meaning of Christ, the Messiah, or Anointed One. It is

He who has been burnt of all impurities, one on whom the power of God has descended, to remain in wisdom, love and truth.

The soul's relation to this nature, if a thing of reality and not of mere profession and belief, must be made known in cell-growth and organic action.

Whereas, I was blind, I now see; I was sick, and I am healed; I was ignorant, and now I am commencing to know; I was weak and enfeebled, and now I am strong and full of power; and blessed above all things else, what has been done unto me I can also do unto others.

This must be the true declaration of each one who has received, and is having developed, that germ whose presence in the soul imparts health, wisdom, unselfishness, virtue and power, as surely as light emanates from the sun.

Sickness of body, selfishness of mind, impurity of heart cannot exist where the order of Christ has established its rule.

Thus we are looking for great signs and wonders, and cannot be deceived, for we know what Christ means, and are trying to demonstrate the nature in our everyday life.

Therefore, we desire to assist in the work of reformation or regeneration, for we now see how it is brought about, and know the darkness at the beginning comprehended not the light.

The light is to come to us as our minds are unfolded, and the method whereby this work is accomplished we will in our little book try to set forth; which we call the "Key," because we know the key to the kingdom of heaven was given to Saint Peter. We have learned what Saint Peter represents. We will give you the benefit, and that we hope the door to the eternal kingdom will be opened for you while it is yet day.

We recognize God in one of His manifold ways as a power going forth which at first appears as nothing, for we cannot see breath or life when it enters a body that He has designed to in time become perfect. As the flower unfolds, we admire it the more, because we behold its beauties and see the nature of God operating through law and order. Then we adore God for His kindness in giving us a mind capable of perception, which faculty we know is the first to be developed, because we find in our study that perception corresponds to Jacob's first son Reuben, and then each son bears a correspondence to the highest work that man can attain unto—that of unfolding the mind as God from the beginning intended, viz. first to be able to gain a knowledge of Him through the outer form or exterior of all that exists, and then to enter into a closer relationship, for He has prepared the way for us to get out of the wilderness that we are now in.

John advances as the forerunner to declare and make ready the way. We find some minds no longer satisfied with feeble symbolism, and cry out as did John, "Make ready the way!"

The shadow of good things must pass away that the sunlight of truth may enter.

Jesus confounded and humbled the wise men by showing them their ignorance. So we find we must confess that we do not know, before we can learn anything.

We propose to lead you to the soul of the Bible, but cannot lead you unless like the wise men in the temple you wish us to tell that which you do not know.

(We have large works that treat on the overshadowing subject.)

The Saint Peter theory as having the keys to the kingdom we now understand, as being necessary to hold us until the Jesus comes to the temple to open the door, (which is done by the faculties being developed,) and in no other way can we enter into the kingdom, but through the door of the human understanding. This is why Jesus confounded the wise men. He came from God, and was the pattern or type for humanity to follow. We cannot know all things until we come in contact with the Logos or speak. The God within speaks when your mind has been built or fashioned to hold the Holy of Holies, as is given in the account of the building of the temple (in 11 Chronicles). Jesus was born of lowly parents. There were no schools for Him; He was compelled to work; but we find Him, nevertheless, in the temple among the so-called wise men. The meaning of Jesus is to save, to make whole, to complete, a germ from the Highest to complete man in the image and likeness of his Creator. It is a principle set as high as God for us to adore and to worship in our lives. We must fast and pray to obtain it; we must overthrow the rule of appetite and emotion, and erect the standard of justice and law. Our greatest enemies are within, and Jesus cannot be born even in the manger.

We begin as truth seekers to know God, and as the mind unfolds we perceive the tree of knowledge. Good and evil, old states and conditions must pass away, for the new Jerusalem is to come. We begin our work in the garden of Eden, and find Adam means the earth; this we cultivate. Eve is the receptive nature in man. Thus we have two natures as dual beings, positive and negative—repulsive and attractive. The mind is the God's greatest work. We deal exclusively with soul or mind. The soul of man was at first conjoined to the soul of a beast, and this is where we begin to reason. In our line of thought we go back to primitive man, follow him up from generation to generation, and find him to-day only partially formed and fashioned in the image of his Creator. We are to be in time a little lower than the angels crowned with majesty and honor.

To go on unfolding the Japhetic or intellectual nature to the exclusion of the Shemitic or spiritual would prove disastrous, and we are now beginning to hear the voice of one crying in the wilderness "Make ready the way!" Jesus at an early age expressed wisdom. He is the embodiment of wisdom. Once, standing in the door of the carpenter's shop He watched a great storm gather which darkened the heavens, and its fury swept down the valley. There were two houses, one it took, for it had been built upon shifting sand, the other, which remained, He noticed had a rock foundation. Therefore, when He grew older, He said to the people who followed Him, "Whosoever heareth these sayings of mine and doeth them, I will liken them unto a wise man, who built his house upon a rock: and the winds blew, and beat upon that house, and it fell not: for it was built upon a rock. And every one that heareth these sayings of mine and doeth them not, shall be likened unto a foolish man, who built his house upon the sand, when the storms came this house fell, and great was the fall thereof."

We see that Jesus remembered all things; He made use of all things; He was alive to all things;

and this is the state that pleases God. We are not alive (in the spirit) but sleeping. The earth has overcome us. We must overcome the earth, Adam. We must cultivate the faculties, and they will in time bring about harmony and perfection. We must not only hear of His sayings but we must do them, or like the man who built his house upon the sand, we will fall far short of what God has designed. To be a little lower than the angels requires us to watch and pray. This we would do if we were wise, but our wisdom is likened unto the doctors in the temple.

The Bible was created by God for the purpose of holding us together in what is called spiritual things; we know the Bible has done its work in this line. We further know that very many minds have unfolded in the intellectual nature and cannot understand the Bible. This we also recognize as a natural state, and as we called for more light, we have obtained it through the channel opened by Jesus, who said: "I go to prepare the way." A small ray has been permitted to shine across our paths blessing us, and we desire to extend the blessing, for we know it is more blessed to give than to receive. We desire to awaken an interest in all who are dissatisfied or restless as we were until we found the golden key to the kingdom of heaven. We recognize the Bible's outer meaning or surface as the husk

which the swine did eat, and the interior or soul of the Bible as the manna sent from heaven. The choice is ours. God has given both freely.

The twelve sons of Jacob represent active agents at work outwardly (in the early history of man), but when the mind has unfolded to perceive the wisdom of God in delivering us out of the land of Egypt and out of the house of bondage, then we read the soul of the Bible and our souls glorify God. We are just commencing to learn of spiritual things, we are at the foot of the golden ladder; we have become as the little child; we have entered the straight and narrow path but we know it leads to the eternal kingdom.

Man does not yet know himself, hence, this state that we call unrest. We will go back to the time of Noah and lead the mind into a new channel of thought (and yet it is as old as the world itself). Noah had three sons, Shem, Ham and Japhet. These three sons are closely related to us because we receive their natures. Shem gives us the nature we call spiritual. It was this line that brought forth David and Jesus. If we desire to become perfect we must unfold this nature.

It is worth all of our time aud study to please God for He tells us to "seek first the highest kingdom, then all things needful shall be added unto us." The Shemitic nature is to be unfolded and then we reach the top of the golden ladder, for heaven is a state of consciousness to be gained here and now, when we know God.

Do you not see great wisdom here displayed? God called us long ago but we were not ready because we could not understand His laws consequently could not obey them. We have been held by the signs and forms, parables and allegories, until our Japhetic nature has been developed and we cry out for more light on our darkened paths. Peter denotes a rock and Jesus said the church was to be built upon this rock which is Reason.

Peter stands ready with the key to open the door into the kingdom when you are prepared to call on him through reason. It will point out to you the true way as, "I am the vine, ye are the branches." It is knowledge that gives us power in all of our undertakings in life, and we put forth every effort to obtain in the material knowledge whereby we may add to our resources but here we are in the nineteenth century often confused, perplexed, and annoyed if questioned as to who is God.

This little work is not to create inharmony, except as Paul said to grieve you in a godly way. Then let us try to understand God for He is our foundation, the Rock of Reason, and we build upon it. We find the names given to God are all expressive of natures separate yet united. We learn and are familiar with God through His names first, and then through His works and ways which denotes His nature in all things. Thus it is pleasure and profit combined that leads us into the kingdom of heaven.

"Except ye become as a little child ye cannot enter the kindgom." Why this statement is true is this: The little child nature is pleasing to God for He said "let the little ones come unto me and forbid them not." The little child nature is not full of pride, selfishness, passion or notions that holds its mind in pervesity. It is the nature that wants to know, to learn, to be taught, to be guided, directed and ruled, as is given by the meanings of law.

Except ye are born from above ye cannot enter into the kingdom of heaven. Why is this true? To be born from above means to know, for above means the head, and we cannot know except as the faculties are developed which bring about a perfect mind.

We must recognize God in creation, for all is His handiwork. The mind of man being His greatest work, it has necessarily taken longer for us to reach the truth in this line of thought than in the Japhetic line. It has taken thousands of years, or since the beginning, to prepare us for the Light of the Logos or Word which was at first shown in man by his ability to think and then to make known his thoughts in words, as the meaning of the Word or Logos is to number and order. As we see it declared in all of the different forms of the universe, every thing in its kind, from the lowest to the highest state, each perfected in its order, so do we recognize the necessary means or method whereby man's mind was to be brought up into a state of knowing its Creator and giving Him the praise and the glory that we often give to man.

The serpent was more subtle than anything God had made. The meaning of the word (to be naked) proves the unadorned state of the mind. As we represent this nature it will be readily seen that it is God's opponent, for it is evil, or unfinished, imperfect, while God is perfection. This low state represented by the serpent is our greatest enemy and requires all of our wisdom and power to subdue and bring it under control. It will be necessary to study the nature of God to become familiar with the working of His divine plan and to perceive the truth in all things. This requires an effort on our part, and, if we read the Bible aright, we will find that God has made provision for this state of transition from lower to higher things. (We care not for the murmur of the multitude should they be pleased to say we are wrong.) The God that we worship in spirit and in truth is the true and living God.

When the earnest seeker finds the truth in relation to the Deity it will have erased from his or her mind a personal God, for these names (new to us) Elohim, Jehovah, and Elshida do the work of establishing our minds as they could not otherwise be established, hence, we overcome a part of the serpent in our nature through a desire to learn of Him who knowing of the desire has given us the low nature represented by the serpent to overcome, and we obey the law which liberates us from the enemy. Adam and Eve represent the positive and negative, creative and receptive powers of the mind. As we advance in this new line of thought we find all things made clear to the mind for it is seeking and finding the truth which sets it free from doubt and fear. Then, full of faith, we go forth to do His bidding for we realize the Master has come and know that the conqueror, truth, reveals all things, that man is not yet ashamed of his nakedness, is still apparent. It is his ignorance, animalism, selfishness, immaturity, and imperfections that still hold him from a consciousness of his Creator. He is immured in matter, (the garden of earthly delight,) and he does not yet reason that these pleasures are not to last; he is simple and ignorant as yet.

This state, which we recognize as death, is to be overcome by experience as the ripened fruit of our search for spiritual things. We know God gave his only begotten Son to save humanity and read the method whereby this state called Son is to be brought into our lives. The meaning of Son is one perfected, one made whole, one in whom all of the faculties have been developed or rounded out, a perfect mind. This state pleases God and this is why He sent His Son that we in time may be the many brethren, Christ the first. We are to follow in His footsteps. By overcoming or resisting in the physical we gain strength, so in the mental, if we overcome we must expect a reward. The great difficulty at first is to watch and pray that we may not send forth one thought in the wrong direction, for the serpent is ever ready to allure us until we have become strong in our determination for spiritual things. We must bear in mind that God is the ruler of a world of intelligence, and when we direct our thoughts to Him through His angelic ministers we will be prepared to receive an answer from Him. But we must turn from the old and enter the new way of thinking and doing, *i.e.* first to know God through his works and ways in creation. Although it is a pleasure, there are many temptations, for we are very apt to follow Japhet instead of Shem in our studies. The Will is the faculty represented by Asher, which means to guide, to direct, to be firm, to go forward, to prosper, to succeed. In the Scriptures we find the will used synonymously with life and soul, thus indicating as man thinketh so is he; or as he wishes so is he drawn toward the same nature outwardly. Man is a dual being, and having in his nature the two opposites he is subject to captivity, until he is established in spiritual things. The Bible contains a mine of wealth. If we are not satisfied or nourished by its outward meaning, remember the pure gold is hidden in the etymology of the Hebrew and Greek.

We have been growing toward this state of wanting to know God from the very first. It could not present itself to us in thought and deed before but it now appeals to our reason and we are not afraid to speak for the truth sustains us.

God would not leave us in the wilderness. Joshua (the same meaning as Jesus) is selected to lead the children of Israel across the Jordan into Canaan.

The children of Israel are those who desire the pure gold. Crossing the Jordan means that we leave or pass away from the lower nature and then we are prepared to enter the promised land —the understanding of law and obedience to truth.

We are told that Joshua commanded the sun and moon to stand still. This is necessary in our work. If we would conquer our enemies we must do what Joshua did, only he represents the outward working of a law, and we learn to know in our natures of the warlike tribes, Philistines, Amorites, Jebusites, Moabites, Hivites, etc., and that these tribes are ruling us. If we would cross the Jordan, we must put them to flight. If we would progress, we must conquer the enemies.

The sun is the outward sign or form of our soul. As the moon shines by reflected light we find it represents the intellect, and knowing the soul is the source and center of life and light to our little world, we realize the command given by Joshua, "Sun, stand thou still on Gibeon, and thou moon in the valley of Ajalon!" for we understand the truth of this statement. We know the intellect often holds us, and we must cry out to be delivered. When the Jesus principle has been established there will be no more contention and doubt; but while the five senses hold us the five kings, Joshua cannot deliver us, and he commands the sun and moon to stand still.

When mental order is brought about, the mind represents as do the heavens a pleasure to behold. In Judah is God known; "His name is great in Israel." Judah means faith, and when we develop this faculty to glorify God, Israel will lead us into heaven or Salem, where the tabernacle is. The meaning of Salem is complete, made perfect and whole. This is also a state to be reached in our unfoldment.

David means one beloved of the Lord, and the psalms that he gave from the fullness of his soul have held us and sustained us as food; but we must awaken to a consciousness as did David, and represent the same state; then we too will be beloved of the Lord.

God is no respecter of persons. He would not have sent His only beloved Son unless He knew we could gain the same state that He represented as being one with Him. He opened the way for us to follow in the direct path straight and narrow, for it leads us unto eternal life.

"What does it profit a man if he gain the whole world and lose his own soul?" Our souls must be saved, and when we turn from the old way of reading the Scriptures and enter the new, then we realize the growth as never before, because we are dealing with axioms.

Let us not grow faint-hearted, for all souls are to be saved. We desire to prove that now is the accepted time. We are told in Gen. 9: 27, Japhet should be enlarged and dwell in the tents of Shem, proving that the Japhetic nature in time would seek the spiritual or Shemitic; but Canaan was to be the servant of servants, proving the Hamitic nature to be the lowest; and our time is wasted when we develop Ham to the exclusion of Shem. Thus it is that we find the Shemitic nature to be the one that God called us to unfold first.

We read that Cain killed Abel. Abel represents the higher spiritual nature of man, and Cain means anger, passion, jealousy. This is the nature that kills Abel—a breath or spirit. Whenever a higher inspiration or desire is not actualized, because of some ruling, earthly, selfish passion or ambition, then it is that Abel cries from the earth to God for vengeance that is sure to come.

And so we find in all the books of the Bible (for it is the history of the human soul), and in each person a state or condition reached in or to be, as states we must pass through before the Sabbath day or state of peace comes, which Sabbath denotes.

There are many mansions prepared for us in our Father's house. According to our stage of soul growth, will we find the mansion that we may enter; but bear in mind, progression is the law, and we are constantly learning in higher things. By obeying His laws and precepts, by having proper respect for all His agencies, we know that God is pleased with us.

We do not find fault with anything that tends to unfold the mind, because God operates in this way to reach us. Even miracles have been used in developing the mind, and we will give a few instances where miracles have been performed. (We quote from a writer who has no belief in theology.) In speaking of miracles, he says he might write a book of miracles were he to relate the hundredth part of all that takes place every year, nay, every day, in Italy—Bohn's "Rome in the Nineteenth Century," edition of 1852. In the second volume, beginning at page 226, there is an account of some Roman miracles; within one month three great miracles happened in Rome. An image of the Virgin opened her eyes. She was carried away, and certain priests who were supposed to have been in her confidence on this occasion were shut up in prison. A Madonna spoke to an old washerwoman to whom she imparted her discontent at being so much neglected, and her chapel left in such a ruinous and dirty condition, while so many other Madonnas, no better than she, had theirs made as fine as hands could make them. This news spread like wildfire, and thousands may be seen every day crowding to this little old chapel about four in the afternoon, the hour at which the Virgin addressed the washerwoman, not only the lower class of people, but crowds of well dressed people and handsome equipages of all sorts. The throng is daily, and presents the appearance of a fair. A chair at the corner of every street which leads to the chapel has a white cloth spread over it with a picture of the Madonna, and a plate is awaiting your donation to beautify her chapel. The luck that has come to this Madonna for opening her mouth has caused disgrace to fall upon the others, and some have gone so far as to say this Madonna was born with a silver spoon in her mouth. As if one Madonna scorned to be outdone by another, there is an old, dirty, cobweby Virgin in the Pantheon which has lately begun to work miracles, and has drawn such crowds to her shrine that an unhappy stranger can scarcely get in to see the building. Italy seems always to have been the land of superstition, and the pagan miracles that are upon record at least equal the Roman Catholic, both in number and absurdity. Every page of Livy and Plutarch abounds with them. Not a year ever passed without two or three oxen speaking, though we never hear any of their sayings. Now even a Madonna but rarely makes use of her tongue, and oxen have entirely given up talking. However, it is a different thing hearing nonsense that was credited years ago, and seeing it before one's eyes; and when I behold crowds flocking to kneel before these talking and winking Madonnas, I cannot help asking myself if this is really the nineteenth century?" This writer goes on to state in the month of February, 1858,, the Virgin Mary appeared at Lourdes to a little peasant girl who could neither read nor write. She was sent to gather brushwood for fuel, for her parents were very poor. She kneeled to pray at the grotto of Massabielle, and all at once the Virgin Mary manifested herself to her, and within fifteen days there were as many as five thousand spectators present in the morning when this little girl (Bernadette Soubirous) came to interview the Virgin. No one ever saw the Virgin except Bernadette. Where there were no signs of water before, a spring of pure clear water came gurgling forth, pouring out a hundred thousand litres a day. Then the spring drew thousands upon thousands of pilgrims every year. Millions of money have been spent there by the pilgrims. The miraculous water is bottled and sent all over Europe, whereever there are Roman Catholics. The church has bought all the property in sight for miles about Lourdes, and it has been improved and made very attractive. A large handsome church, costing two millions of francs, has been built from the contributions of pilgrims, and the miracle business is in a most flourishing condition there now. In September, 1877, the miracles of one pilgrimage which began in August is given. There were about twelve hundred pilgrims upon two railway trains, one following immediately behind the other. Twenty-four were healed; the lame, blind and deaf were cured, and their names given. The number of pilgrims who arrived at Lourdes during the week ending Sept. 22, 1877, according to the "Palerin" (newspaper) of that week, was five thousand six hundred and five. The writer further adds it is the believers who make the miracles, and not the miracles that make the believers. Miracles are always possible wherever the people are sufficiently ignorant and superstitious. The first condition for the happening of a miracle is the existence of believers.

The Protestant church, which embraces the most intelligent portion of mankind, says there has been no miracle in the world since the time of Jesus. Centuries ago miracles were abundant, because people were ignorant and could be made to believe in them, but nowadays miracles are generally out of style. We would not quote from this writer unless it were to take a lesson from witchcraft and miracles, as we do from all things which tend to hold the mind and impress us with wonder workings.

It is the manner in which we see, or take from any or all things that are sent to open our eyes, or the blind state. Remembering that we were once dumb, it is not at all strange to us that God has prepared ways and means to operate upon the dumb state or beast that often holds us in the earth.

The plan for our salvation is the one that we know the least about; and yet we think that the name Christian is sufficient to cover our multitude of sins. Do we not see in the churches people who are as ignorant of God and His laws as we find outside the church?

God abominates ignorance. It is darkness, the opposite to God who is light.

Were we not made to see these things we could not enter the vineyard to do our work. But when we cast our eyes over the world and see on every hand distress. Rich and poor are here alike, for God is the Maker of all. Then it creates in our mind activity, motion; the power of God enters into us, and we must tell the truth.

There is a way unto salvation, but it will not come to us; we must seek it. Then we hear the words, "hide not your light under a bushel, etc.," and we will try to reach one soul, for we know there is more rejoicing over one sinner who repenteth than over the ninety and nine just ones.

What does repentance consist of? We must understand that we are doing a wrong before we can repent. While we are satisfied with our state we cannot repent, because we do not know that we are wrong in being held by other minds besides our own. We are wrong—other minds cannot repent for us, other minds cannot expand for us, other minds cannot atone for us. God calls us to Him, "All who are weary come unto me." Perhaps you have not thought it was you; you may think if you are in the church it means the church, or the way to Him is through the church. If you are yet helpless, it may be that you cannot depend upon yourself, but do you ask the church to supply you with material food, or do you expect that your bills will be paid by or through the church?

Remember we are only reasoning now, together. Jesus called the twelve on the mount and this is what we desire to do. The mount is a state for us to reach in the enfoldment of the mind, where we can reason with our disciples (or faculties) and here we find a Godly work to perform because Jesus opened the way and whatever He has done we may do. Therefore you see we are only trying to draw you up higher, and again, as Paul said, If we confuse or annoy you let it be for a time only, because if you are capable of reasoning for yourself you will find God within. "Ask what ye will in my name that will I give unto you."

Then if your mind is ruffled because you are in the church and cannot see the wisdom of God in all things, stir up the soil in your nature and perhaps you will find yourself growing. When in time you weigh the words of Him who prepared the way unto salvation and you will find your mind stronger because you are doing the work for yourself, whereas formally you had it done for you.

On the same principle do we find the physical supplies us with strength. Use all of your powers. We cannot afford to slumber or sleep away this life. God is activity, motion; we must take hold to live. "Man does not live by bread alone, but by every word which proceedeth out of the mouth of God."

Here you may see that a mind prepared to draw from the fountain head does not live on the husk. The true bread of life is in your soul; you must put forth the energy that God has given to you and be guided by Him who tells you to ask what ye will in His name.

Then you will grow and the tree of life will flourish because the roots have touched the living spring. It is hard to part with old friends, but harder to separate ourselves from notions or ideas that have rooted themselves into our very lives. If we watch and pray (when once we desire to repent), then the angels will assist us and the battle is won. Then said he unto me: "Fear not Daniel; (judgment) for from the first day that thou didst set thine heart to understand, and to chasten thyself before thy God, thy words were heard and I am come for thy words." You see an angel comforts Daniel, and although he was in the lions' den, the beasts did not devour him. Judgment will always sustain you when God is the judge.

What greater miracle than this can we ask, for we read that Nebuchadnezzar, King of Babylon, sent for Daniel and found him in matters of wisdom and understanding ten times better than all the magicians and astrologers that were in all his realm.

But the king was not at first ready to have Daniel brought to him. The magicians satisfied him. The time came that he had to call upon Daniel, and so it may be in our lives; we may not be quite ready to have judgment passed upon us. Have we yet called upon Daniel (judgment)? You see the Bible is the history of our souls, and we cannot afford to lose time in conjecture with the magicians—we want the truth.

We know that He numbers and orders according to grade. Perhaps in this way you may find the grade to which you belong, and as you learn of the method whereby God calls us higher, you too will call upon His name and receive what you ask for, provided you do not ask amiss.

Satan himself is transformed into an angel of light. When we use judgment, then it is that Satan is changed from evil to good. (Evil and good are the same in the etymology of the

Hebrew). Thus we know that man ought always to pray that the mind may be established in that which is good. We do not coerce—our work does not admit of it. We say stand by thyself; with God to guide thee, there is no ill that can betide thee.

A writer has declared that truth should be shouted from the housetops; but are we as yet ready to receive it from the pages of a quiet little book? We know in time all will see face to face because it is written in our history. 1 John iv. We find those who speak of the world are in the world; it is the world who heareth. We are of God; he that knoweth God heareth us; he that is not of God heareth not us. Hereby know we the spirit of truth, and the spirit of error. He that loveth not, knoweth not God; for God is love. If we love one another, God dwelleth in us, and His love is perfected in us. Whosoever shall confess that Jesus is the Son of God, God dwelleth in him and he in God.

We have no fear, for perfect love casteth out fear. We love the human family as a whole and desire to do His will, for it is He who hath sent us to bind as frontlets before the eyes His commandments. The first commandment we do not obey. Deut. xxxii:1-4: "Give ear, O ye heavens and I will speak: and hear, O earth, the words of my mouth. He is the Rock, his work is perfect:

for all his ways are judgment: a God of truth and without iniquity, just and right is he. He kept Jacob as the apple of his eye after he found him in the wilderness or desert land. The Lord led Jacob, but he tells us it was him alone who led him, there was no strange gods with him. Then Jacob was fed with honey from the rock and the pure blood of the grape."

Jeshurun forsook God who made him and lightly esteemed the Rock of salvation. This state did not please God and He said: "I will hide my face from thee Jeshurun and see what your end shall be." For the nation was void of counsel, neither was there any understanding in them. Their vine is of the vine of Sodom, and of the fields of Gomorrah; their grapes are grapes of gall, their clusters are bitter. Their wine is the poison of dragons, and the cruel venom of asps.

Is not this laid up in store with me, and sealed up among my treasures? To me belongeth vengeance and recompense. Their foot shall slide in due season; for the day of their calamity is at hand, and the things that come upon them, make haste.

"For the Lord shall judge his people, and he shall say, where is their rock in whom they trusted? where are their gods? I kill, and I make alive; I wound and I heal. See now that I, even

I, am he, and there is no god with me. For I lift up my hand to heaven, and say I live forever. If I whet my sword I take hold on judgment."

We are told to set our hearts unto all the words that Moses gave to us, for they are not vain. They are our life and our days shall be prolonged in the land whither we go to possess. We must cross the Jordan to the land here promised, and find that all our sins' are forgiven, even though they be as scarlet, if we are baptized through His word which is law.

Therefore we must obey the law in all things, There are mediums in our midst who are doing the work for some minds, or what witchcraft and magic has done for others, but we have developed Daniel and find that we belong to the tribe of Israel and cannot serve false gods. We know that God is light and we reason in this way: If God sent His only begotten Son to save humanity and then gave us the Bible as the history of the race, we should be willing as Jacob was to be led out of the wilderness, and then we are fed upon the honey and blood of the grape, for we recognize God as all powerful, and because we have no false gods to take from the true and living God, He gives us judgment and we can discern the truth.

By the breaking of the Bread of Life the whole multitude are fed. The thoughts are here represented as the multitude, and you may see God's wisdom in holding your mind by loaves and fishes until you are ready to leave the false gods that now hold you. As Paul said if the epistle grieved you to godliness it has done its work, for this is His plan to lead us to salvation. Truth is stranger than fiction and the beauties of creation are on every hand were it not for our cold-hearted selfishness we need not take our flight in winter, but obey His laws and live. Law is the manifestation of the power of God through forms. Mind is the product of soul-power made known through the faculties, and by its highest use we become united in consciousness with that Supreme Being whom law points out, and by whose instrumentalities we are forever and forever to be led and ruled. The command to love the Lord thy God with all thy heart, mind, might and strength, and thy neighbor as thyself, has not been understood, consequently, we could not live up to it. It is to have no life but in the knowledge of the laws of God, obedience to them, and the giving of all that one has or is, that the brothers's soul may be unfolded. Since creation's dawn upon this planet, there has been but One who obeyed the law, but we would not feel satisfied with our life work unless we saw a tending toward this state, for we know what has been done by One, even the Son of God, may be done by all. He was the first of many brethren yet to be.

We become interested in all souls who are searching for the truth. Patience and perseverance overcome all difficulties; it requires these two requisites in our nature. If we would succeed lay aside all that conflicts, or those ideas or notions that have held your mind from His presence. (1 Cor. 1-29). Let us determine (as did Paul) not to know anything among us, save Jesus Christ and him crucified. If we want to demonstrate the spirit of power our faith cannot be in men, but in the power of God. We are told and feebly realize the hidden wisdom which God ordained before the world. This it is that he desires us to possess. He tells us had we known it Jesus would not have been crucified for He was the Lord of Glory. Again He tells us, " Eye hath not seen, nor ear heard, neither have entered into the heart of man the things which God hath prepared for them that love him. " But God hath revealed them unto us by His Spirit; for the Spirit searcheth all things, yea, the deep things of God.

God works upon the mind of man, building it higher and still higher that he may commune with his Maker in spirit and in truth, for the mind in time becomes established and it knows God and how the desire or prayer is to be answered for it is sent direct to Him who has prepared the way. This is soul communion. We are not in a state to commune with God through His angelic messengers, until we are ready to take up our cross and follow Him. The faculty represented by Benjamin must be developed for we cannot understand our Father's plan until we have brought forth conscientiousness.

As Benoni was born into the world through great suffering and pain, so through the labor and travail of the soul is this faculty evolved which condemns us for ignorance and imperfection. Then through contrition and repentance we are brought into submission to a higher law of thought and action. On the same principle is it that we cultivate the soil; we must plough deep and harrow well to reap a bountiful harvest, (all things being equal.) So do we find some souls more advanced or cultivated than others, and these principles being offered to such a soul (one prepared) proves the seed has fallen upon good ground as in the parable. It is the eye that sees and the ear that hears that benefits by the inner meaning or soul of the Bible. We are told that Mary brought forth Jesus and she knew not man. Was it a miracle? If so, can it be explained? We will give you the true meaning of Mary. The Virgin Mary represents the female, receptive state which was first personified in Eve, and through which all higher mental power has come, when it has been impregnated with germs from unseen realms above. A virgin signifies that which has been set apart, consecrated to a special purpose. Mary denotes fullness and rebellion. We know the state that brings forth Jesus Christ is a state in the soul which rebels at the rule of symbols and signs and refuses all states or conditions which are ruling the earth to-day through physical, intellectual and moral unfoldment as we find religious or secular things given or disseminated to the people through the churches. Mary rebels and the Holy Ghost comes upon this state of the soul, the power of the Most High overshadows this state and the Son of God is brought forth that which is holy and good. Joseph, the husband of Mary, represents, as his name indicates, the masculine positive, organizing constructive power of the human soul. This state of mind does not know, cannot understand that interior receptive condition which Mary personifies. We are through with the signs and forms or else we could not understand the mission of Jesus the Christ. Christ declared to Nicodemus that until other souls had been begotten and born from above (which is the mind unfolded that it may know and understand spiritual things) we could not apprehend the laws of the kingdom called the highest or heavenly. "Marvel not that

I said unto thee, ye must be born again," St. John iii :7, and Christ knowing of our credulity left these words that we might in time read and understand: "If ye believe not what I tell you concerning earthly things, how shall ye believe if I tell you of heavenly things ? No man hath ascended up to heaven but he that came down from heaven, even the Son of man which is in heaven." The soul is a part of deity, consequently Jesus, as the Son, or first fruit, came down from heaven. This is the language but it cannot fully express the action; for the soul must, like Mary, be prepared or rebel against the confusion of ideas and notions and want the truth, for the highest overshadowing cannot come until the virgin is prepared to receive the Word of God. (This is the seed that falls upon good ground). Prepare then the way unto salvation; many are called but few are chosen, for the Virgin Mary state has not come to the soul. The many brethren are yet to be, and the world is now in a state to receive them for the selfishness and cold-heartedness is creating inharmony and injustice. The church militant is the church triumphant. We must find the true church before we can have peace. The mind must be in a harmonious state and this state cannot exist separate and apart from the whole truth. Jesus came to save the world from the chaotic state that we are now in, but we must do our part to give' birth to the Prince of the World, then the principality and the power is ours, for that which is born is called good, the Son of God. The meaning of son is to have life, that which has been gradually formed, constructed or completed. Then a Son of God is a soul that has been gradually formed and when completed it knows its Father and obeys His will.

The oneness which indicates a union is to be brought to every soul, for we are upon our journey toward the heavenly kingdom and it depends wholly upon our will. Shall we take the straight and narrow path that leads to salvation or light which illumines the mind? (as fast as we turn toward it, the truth). Or do we prefer the chaotic state, which is darkness or death? for it is the opposite of life and light. We would urge the former but if the soil is not prepared our desire could not be fulfilled.

We, who are permitted to work in the vineyard, must do our work according to the command that we love one another as He hath loved us, and greater love can no man show than this, that he is willing to lay down his life to save his fellowman. In times of war when men are called upon to save their country they respond. Although man may be an infidel he will sacrifice himself for his country's good, but this is a feeble state crying out for liberty. The liberty that comes to the soul when the mind is unfolded is the highest form of liberty, because it is the truth that sets us free from ignorance, which is sinful to the eye that can perceive it. "You shall know the truth and the truth shall set you free." We realize all religion to be a step toward the great center or Creator. This we desire to reach in the way that is good. The mind must be unfolded before it can be operated upon by the higher orders. The truth will shine at times more brightly than at others and when the desire to know God is uppermost in your mind be true to the desire and place yourself in such relation (mentally) that the angels may impress you, that you may be led into green pastures and beside the still waters. As your soul is restored you will recognize the higher powers are leading you, keeping in mind to be a Son of God and heir to the highest kingdom, you must please your Father in all things. This will be your saving power for you cannot serve two masters. You will find the straight and narrow path at first difficult to follow, but it leads you up and on in ways of pleasantness, where all your paths are peace you will find truth stranger than fiction the glorious stories of old will be verified in your everyday life. You, like the beloved Son, will know that it is more blessed to give than to receive, and as you gather the gems, so will you scatter them. The soil is being prepared. We must obtain the word of God that we may sow in due season, for the harvest will be in keeping with the well-tilled soil; and He who watches over all and calls himself Lord of the harvest is the one we strive to please. Not as those who worship in temples built by man have we fear. We always rejoice giving no offence in anything, that the ministry be not blamed. By pureness, by knowledge, by long-suffering, by kindness, by the Holy Ghost, by love unfeigned. By the word of truth, by the power of God, by the armor of righteousness on the right hand and on the left. As unknown, and yet well known; as dying, and, behold, we live; as chastened, and not killed. As sorrowful yet always rejoicing; as poor, yet making many rich; as having nothing, and yet possessing all things. O ye Corinthians, our mouth is open unto you, our heart is enlarged. For we are the temple of the living God; as God hath said I will dwell in them, and walk in them; and I will be their God and they shall be my people. Wherefore come out from among them, and be ye separate, saith the Lord, and touch not the unclean thing, and I will receive you. And I will be a Father unto you, and ye shall be my sons and daughters, saith the Lord Almighty—2 Cor. 6: 3, 6, 7, 9; 10, 11, 16, 17, 18. Paul wrote to his dearly beloved, the Macedonians, and rejoiced that his epistle or letter had caused them sorrow because the sorrow was turned to repentance, and he called it a godly manner, for godly sorrow worketh repentance to salvation not to be repented of; but the sorrow of the world worketh death. The letter was written by Paul to establish in the minds of the Macedonians faith, and that his greatest desire was to bring them nearer to God. So with this little work sent out to perform its mission as the key to the kingdom. It may offend some but we shall rejoice if by it ye are made sorry after a godly manner, that ye may receive damage by us in nothing, for this kind of sorrow worketh repentance not to be repented of. We have gone through the battle, we have fought the good fight and we know whereof we speak. We speak all things to you in truth and trust that you may be prepared to receive it, that your joy may be full. We thank God who has put the same earnest care into our heart as was given to Titus, for we, like him, have accepted the exhortation and come forward of our own accord to arrest your minds in the whirl of our modern Babylon. As the tribes of Judah availed themselves of the permission given by Cyrus to return to their own country after the captivity, so we desire faith, which is Judah, to be restored and lean upon the One who calls us unto Him as the way to salvation. Let us be free in our thoughts to range at will over all that has been and now is preparing the mind to establish the true temple, the real temple, the temple that is built by Solomon, (a state of peace) for the indwelling of the Holy Spirit. This we find as recorded in 2 Book of Chronicles the dimensions of the temple, furniture of the temple, induction of the ark. Solomon blesseth the temple. His prayer at the consecration of the temple, his sacrifices, God's promises to him and Solomon's buildings, etc., speak in language plain to those who can hear that it was God's pleasure to have the Bible written as it has been to hold us together as a conserving power until the mind was prepared as is given in Chronicles, that the place called the interior or ark of the covenant could be discerned by man through the unfolding of his faculties, and his mind capable to reason and commune with the true and living God. This has required time and time is still necessary to unfold the mind of the masses, but we have, like Paul, advanced the epistle that may grieve you, but still it is to do its godly work. Science unfolds the mind, law establishes it. Then let God who is the maker of law send into your mind the light that is to light every man who cometh into the world in darkness. And yet some of us who are in the darkened state called Egypt, cannot see, because we have a heart like

Pharaoh's hardened and we refuse to let our thoughts turn in the right direction. Pharaoh wanted miracles performed before he would listen to the law giver, Moses, and so it is to-day; we will call for any and all things before we will bow to the law, putting off until to-morrow as did Pharaoh saying if the Lord will only take away those things that we do not admire. We must admit our perverse nature holds us, but if ye repent and overcome the kingdom of heaven is at hand. It is within reach of us as God's children; then let us worship from the true temple and please Him who hath sent the law first through Moses, and then engraves them upon the tablets of our minds. Gad (memory) serves us now and we cannot forget what he has told us. Then Asher (the will) is obedient to his Father and we are happy because we are loved by the Father for we obey His commands. Deut. iv: 9: "Only take heed to thyself, and keep thy soul diligently, lest thou forget the things which thine eyes have seen, and lest they depart from thy heart all the days of thy life; but teach them to thy sons and thy sons' sons." As the voice was heard in the midst of the fire in Horeb, so may we look for the truth in the midst of our trials (if we are not like Pharaoh). As the Lord spoke out of the midst of the fire so will he again speak to those who hear his word, for he desires us to get through with the signs and forms, the likeness of anything he tells us not to worship even the sun, moon and stars. He tells us not to serve false gods. He has brought us out of the iron-furnace, even out of Egypt, to be unto Him a people of inheritance as we are this day. If we persist in our hard-heartedness we are to be scattered among the heathen and serve gods the work of men's hands which have no life, for they cannot see, or hear, or eat, or smell, and they are an abomination to the Lord our God, who has brought us out of the land of Egypt and out of the house of bondage. Out of heaven He made thee, hear His voice, that He may instruct thee. For the voice as of consciousness (Benjamin) must deliver thee to thy Creator. It may appear to you that the whole world is right and this little (apparently) insignificant book is wrong (perhaps constructed upon supposition) but we will turn to the tables as Moses gave us the law engraved on tablets of stone, so do we find in our hearts the truth written as ordained by Him who constructed the law and it is through our study of the Law of Laws that we are enabled to send forth this little weapon of defence for we are sustained in the work through the laws of God. We desire to place you in the way that in time you may go forth and do His bidding. The city built upon a hill cannot be hid; neither should men light a candle and place it under a bushel, but in a candlestick where all may see and glorify their Father who art in heaven. Be earnest if you would know God, for to see God is to perceive His laws; to conform to them is to obey Him. This understanding is the only lasting source of power; and all laws are alike divine whether governing the physical, intellectual or spiritual nature of man. Law means to lay a foundation, to put straight, to regulate, to point out, to teach, to guide, to rule.

The times now are not greatly in advance of the time these words were written.

The Acts Chap. 28: 26-27 saying, "Go unto this people, and say, Hearing ye shall hear, and shall not understand; and seeing ye shall see and not perceive. For the heart of this people is waxed gross, and their ears are dull of hearing, and their eyes have they closed, lest they should see with their eyes and hear with their ears and understand with their hearts and should be converted and I should heal them. Think you the miraculous water at Lourdes has the saving power that is within your own soul that God has given to each of his children when they obey His laws and commandments, first as they were given to Moses and now in the constitution of man speak to him that he may know good from evil, right from wrong, that he may cleave to one and hate the other, then he transforms the one he hates,

Satan, into an angel of light for he knows that all things were created for a wise purpose and the least should be greatest as it bows around the throne of God, for no flesh shall glory until it serves its Master.

"All things shall fade and pass away, but my word shall remain with you forever."

My word wherein thou hast been instructed proves the certainty of all things. Japhet is enlarged but Japhet must dwell in the tents of Shem before we can come into an understanding of God.

The Turk, the Roman Catholic, and the Protestant each think they are right and so they are; but progression is God's law and to remain in the wilderness displeases Him. Thus we know unless we advance in knowledge we are not pleasing to our Father. There is an incentive or motive power that urges us on, and we know that God leads us, for it is the straight and narrow path we tread.

To investigate the foundation of our beliefs as a rule we will find that we know very little of them except as we are led by other minds. As the world is made up of many men, so do we find their various minds have led them into byways and ditches, but now God calls and tells us to come in, the table is spread, the feast awaits us. St. Matthew xv: 7. Ye hypocrites, well did Esaias prophesy of you, saying, "This people draweth nigh unto me with their mouths and honoreth me with their lips; but their heart is far from me. But in vain do they worship me, teaching for doctrines the commandments of men."

Jesus asked Peter if he was yet without understanding and it would be well if we should question ourselves, Are we not drawing unto God with our mouth? Are we not worshipping in vain? Is our heart not far from God? Have we the faith represented by the woman of Canaan who cried out to Jesus to save her daughter who was possessed of a devil. He told her it was not meet to cast the children's bread to the dogs, and yet she was willing to eat the crumbs that fell from the rich man's table and because of her faith her daughter was made whole.—St. Matt. xv: 21.

It is faith we admire in others, but lack faith in ourselves because Judah has not been developed Abraham represents this faculty developed. He was willing to give up Isaac. We read in Gen. xxii: 9: Abraham built an altar and laid the wood in order and bound Isaac his son, and laid him on the altar upon the wood. And Abraham stretched forth his hand and took the knife to slay his son.

And the angel of the Lord called him out of heaven. and said, Abraham, Abraham! and he said, Here am I. And he said, Lay not thine hand upon the lad, neither do thou anything unto him;

for now I know that thou fearest God, seeing thou hast not withheld thy son, thine only son from me.

And Abraham lifted up his eyes and looked, and behold, behind him a ram caught in a thicket by his horns; and Abraham went and took the ram, and offered him up for a burnt offering in the stead of his son.

God told Abraham because he was willing to give his son; he would multiply and bless his seed which should be as the stars of heaven. The name, (Isaac) means pleasure, joy, laughter, delight. Now God tried Abraham to see how strong his faith was, and when He asked that Isaac be sacrificed and Abraham was willingly preparing to give him, then the ram as a substitute was sent in time for God was not going to have Isaac given bodily. This story represents the working of the mental principles or faculties. In life we are held by the joys, laughter, pleasure and delights of the world. They keep us from God and truth. Not that it is wrong to keep Isaac with us, but like Abraham, if we desire the blessings given by God, we must be willing also to separate ourselves from the earthly pleasure and joy to receive the highest reward. The ram represents strength and power, it signifies a shoot or horn which is a symbol of a higher state being brought to the mind, a consciousness of spiritual joys. In the thicket represents the wild, prolific growth arising from our lower nature into which God has entered as a shoot or power, because, we are through faith in the soul, willing to give up our choicest in the earth (or Isaac).

God works this way to build up the mind. We follow him in his works. Faith is the guiding star to rule and direct us into a knowledge of God. Those who possess the strongest faith must be nearer to Abraham as their father for he was to be the father of many. The father or cause of elevation, and all the nations of the earth were to be blessed, because he obeyed the voice of God. Do not forget that we are dealing with facts. (You may not see as clearly now as you will in time.) If you determine to know or have the faith that Abraham represents then you will be blessed and the blessing will prove more wonderful than any miracle that could be performed, for you will be able to read aright the book of nature, which is God. As you read it all things are manifest, for God is in you operating through law and order. We know why the Bible tells us that man should read as he runs. The book is open, nature reveals all things. The spirit discerneth all things, it is the letter that killeth; therefore, if we desire to liberate our spirit that it may penetrate all things, we must go about it in an orderly way and unfold. If Dan (judgment) has been developed and we have the desire to know God then we read aright. Make a wise selection of some teacher that has been more fully developed than yourself. For a time be a pupil with the desire to become a teacher. It will not be long until you find yourself absorbing all that your teacher has to give, and you may ask questions the teacher cannot answer, for you have proved faithful. Those who are faithful over a few things God has said He would make ruler over many. He now tells you to enter into the joys of His kingdom.

The joys of the Lord are all ready prepared. We find the Lord of Creation or Lord of the Harvest is consciousness. Why can we not enter into the joys? Because we are not conscious of the way though all things tend toward it. But it is left for man to reason or to unfold his mind when he may by so doing be a little lower than the angels. God will crown him with blessings and honor. Man has the opportunity to reach the state that we know Jesus represents. One with God Jesus could do nothing without His Father. We admire his advanced mind, and yet only look on and admire, which brings these words to our remembrance.

Galatians iii : 1 : "O Foolish Galatians, who hath bewitched you, that ye should not obey the truth, before whose eyes Jesus Christ hath been evidently set forth, crucified among you? This only would I learn of you. Receive ye the Spirit by the works of the law, or by the hearing of faith? Are ye so foolish? Having begun in the Spirit, are ye now made perfect by the flesh? Have ye suffered so many things in vain? if it be yet in vain.

He therefore that ministereth to you the Spirit and worketh miracles among you, doeth he it by the works of the law or by the hearing of faith?

Know ye therefore that they which are of faith, the same are the children of Abraham. And the scriptures, foreseeing that God would justify the heathen through faith, preached before the gospel unto Abraham saying, In thee shall all nations be blessed."

It was given to Abraham to demonstrate faith. The Law was given to Moses to hold us until our minds were ready or as we read in Gal. iii :19, Till the seed should come to whom the promise was made; and it was ordained by angels in the hand of a mediator. Further, now a mediator is not a mediator of one, but God is one. Is the law then against the promises of God? God forbid. The law was our school-master to bring us unto Christ, that we might be justified by faith.

But after that faith is come, we are no longer under a school-master, for if we be in Christ then are we Abraham's seed and heirs according to promise. If you can understand the importance of faith and desire to embrace it you are a descendant of Abraham. Test your faith and then you will know, for the blessings will be bestowed upon you. Paul tells Peter he is afraid he has bestowed labor in vain upon him. He tells us we observe days, and months, and times and years, but he fears we do not observe the fullness of this time when God has sent His Son into our hearts, crying, Abba, Father!

When this state comes to the soul we are no more a servant, but a Son, and if a Son, then an heir of God through Christ.

"Am I therefore become your enemy because I speak the truth?—Gal. iv: 16.

Tell me, ye that desire to be under the law, do ye not hear the law?"—Gal. xxi.

Abraham had two sons, the one by a bond-maid the other by a free woman. He who was of the bondwoman was born after the flesh, he of the free woman was by promise. Now we are the brethren of Isaac and of promise, for we find the truth in relation to the Bible account of the handmaid or bondwoman. Hagar belonged to the earth, or was lower than Sarah, which her name implies (to wander and flee), while Sarah means (to establish in order, placing in rows, a power that adjusts and presides.) Thus we find in our study that this story of Abraham having two wives was necessary for us to look upon as all the rest of the Bible as the means of holding the mind of man, until the high priest, Melchizedek, meaning the king of the just, should come forth and establish his rule for the mind is now prepared to continually offer up on the altar which was said to be in the plain of Mamre, Gen. xiii: 18, but which we find to be strength, by which we may overcome all the lower conditions in our nature and turning our thoughts to God we gain renewed strength as we advance for we realize now why Abraham was called to battle. The nature called the animal must be subdued. We go to battle again and again for Cain in the beginning represented this low state that some of us have not yet controlled. Cain is called a Lord murderer. It is this nature, Cain, that holds us in the earth. God did not want Cain's offering. Neither does he to-day, but Abel's offering was acceptable, for he is spoken of as a keeper of sheep, and he gave of the firstlings of his flocks. The sheep are spoken of as firstlings, because the meaning of firstling is something begotten and born whose nature is not to be changed, proving God is pleased with a perfect state.

Cain killed Abel, but the highest must feed the lowest. The work goes on in the mental states and conditions by which we are surrounded.

When the Cain has been brought up and Shem rules, then the freedom of the will is exercised and

directed into the highest channel. "The light is slowly coming," although we see the blind leading the blind, and know that they will all fall into the ditch; still the survival of the fittest is assured, for the promise is made to the seed of Abraham. If you desire to find the truth, and be led through faith, then do as we have done, seek, for the door will be opened, but you know it will not open until you knock.

It is the germ of the nature we call God within our souls that wants to be freed. It has tired of the signs and forms, parables and allegories; it has absorbed all the life or nourishment that they contained. Religion is now dry as a husk; therefore, we hunger and thirst for righteousness, and know somewhere there is food called the Bread of Life or Manna; it is sent from heaven. Heaven is a state of consciousness. We try to bring you face to face with the truth, and all who cry out as did Saul of old shall be delivered.

All the work that has been going on and now exists has been to bring us where we can see that the son of the bondwoman cannot be heir. It is the son of the freewoman. Gal. iv: 31.

So then, brethren, we are not children of the bondwoman, but of the free. Gal. v: 1. Stand fast, therefore, in the liberty wherewith Christ hath made us free, and be not entangled again with the yoke of bondage.

Paul wrote from Athens, and said he found an altar with this inscription, "To the unknown God whom ye ignorantly worship; him do I adore."

Don't you think Paul would have as good cause in this latter day to say that we ignorantly worship?

But we have every advantage now to know. The Holy Ghost saith, to-day if ye will hear His voice, harden not your hearts as in the day of temptation or provocation in the wilderness, when your fathers tempted me, proved me, and saw my works forty years; wherefore I was grieved with that generation, and said, They do always err in their heart, and they have not known my ways: so I sware in my wrath, They shall not enter into my rest. Take heed, brethren, least there be in any of you an evil heart of unbelief in departing from the living God. But exhort one another while it is called to-day, lest any of you be hardened through the deceitfulness of sin.

We find the meaning of sin is a missing of the mark, a state that is changeable, a nature that cannot endure, unripe or immature. You see God is not pleased with this state. He tells us to exhort one another while it is yet day, for we may depart from Him through sin. How can we tell whether we have an evil heart or not, when we do not know God or the Holy Ghost who tells us to hear the voice if our hearts are not hardened. We are in the wilderness where our fathers were, and God is grieved and said they always erred in their hearts, for they have not known me.

The meaning of wilderness is (turning to the mind), a state that is not yet harmonized, but is being prepared to banish the tempter and receive through affliction judgment, the Logos or reason. There must be a revolving and turning before there can be love and harmony introduced into the mind, one must be stirred to the innermost depths of the mind in the state called a wilderness.

The ram came through the thicket or growth of mental disorder, and so God is at work in the wilderness, trying to prepare our minds for law and order to be established, instead of the ungodly state we find to-day, or the wilderness where our fathers were when God said you do not know me.

First Timothy, sixth verse: "But they that will be rich fall into temptation, and a snare, and into many foolish and hurtful lusts, which drown men in destruction and perdition; for the love of money is the root of all evil; which while some coveted after they have erred from the faith, and pierced themselves through with many sorrows; but thou, O man of God, flee these things, and follow after righteousness, godliness, faith, love, patience, meekness. Fight the good fight of faith, whereunto thou art also called, and hast performed a good profession before many witnesses. Charge them that are rich in this world that they be not high-minded, nor trust in uncertain riches, but in the living God, who giveth us richly all things to enjoy; that they do good, that they be rich in good works, ready to distribute, willing to communicate, laying up in store for themselves a good foundation against the time to come, that they may lay hold on eternal life."

Eternal life is here and now, when we understand life's work, or the orderly method of God in creation. God gives us ways and means as perfect in their appointments to our salvation as law and order manifest themselves in their relations. If we are not fully prepared to see, in other words, Rheuben, the first faculty has not been developed. Let us strive to come into an understanding of God through His works and ways. He wants us to unfold all the faculties of the mind. As this is the time, to-day, that the Lord hath appointed for us to enter into the covenant, let us not be of that generation that grieved Him, He who so patiently watches over us, and who tells us to exhort one another daily while it is called to-day, for God knows our weaknesses. We are told if we will hold steadfast to the end we shall be made partakers of Christ. The meaning of Christ is a soul that has been brought forth through the trials and tribulations that have been placed upon it to soften its nature that it may be prepared to receive the Word of God. Christ has been called the first born of many brethren yet to be, for in Christ we find the fulfillment of all the laws and commandments, types, symbols and prophesies. King David marks a state in the mind when it recognizes God through the proper channel, and he tells the angels to bless the Lord, those who excel in strength, that do his commandments, hearkening unto the voice of God.

David is beloved of the Lord (begotten, sent), a state of the mind that must sing praises unto its God, for it realizes God's mercy endureth forever. The temple is built by Solomon (peaceful). We build the mind from a low to a higher state when we find the Bible has a soul, and through its rightful meaning we come in contact with God's greatest handiwork, THE MIND OF MAN.

And we declare unto you glad tidings, how that the promise which was made unto the fathers God hath fulfilled the same unto us their children, in that He hath raised up Jesus again as it is also written in the second. "Thou art my son: this day have I begotten thee." The Acts xiii: 21-31. When we see a soul whose apparel is all virtue, wisdom and power, whose every product in word and deed puts upon itself a form adapted to the necessities of the highest humanity, whose garments are like the ones we know He wore, colored or dyed in affliction, this soul will represent itself as a Jesus.

There will be no need to advertise the Messiah has come, but we will wait patiently for the coming of Christ in humanity, which constitutes a perfect mind. This state is called *My Son*. It pleases the Father, for the faculties are developed, and the mind, like David's, sing praises to God its Creator.

The temple is here finished, and peace is brought by Solomon. The interior court where the Holy of Holies is kept is the ark. The meaning of ark is the highest place for the sacred manna (in the soul) where His word sustains us. And Solomon said he put the covenant of the Lord that he made with the people of Israel into this ark. 11 Chron. vi: 37-38.

Yet if they bethink themselves in the land whither they are carried captive, and turn and pray unto thee in the land of their captivity, saying, "We have sinned; we have done amiss, and have dealt wickedly;" if they return to thee with all their heart and with all their soul in the land of their captivity, whither they have carried them captives, and pray toward their land, which thou gavest unto their fathers, and toward the city which thou hast chosen, and toward the house which I have built for thy name, then hear thou from the heavens, even from thy dwelling-place, their prayer and their supplications, and maintain their cause, and forgive thy people which have sinned against thee.

A prayer made from this place will be answered. We must consider the difference between knowing and thinking that we know. The meaning of thought is to number, to reckon, to complete. You see we must know how to pray from this place that Solomon has built.

"Hear thou from the heavens." We find the meaning of heaven to be a state that is perfect, finished, blest, made whole, completed, established, extended, uplifted, fashioned or wrought. We see the wisdom of God in concealing the true meaning of the Bible until now. We could not have understood before the meaning, and we find even now man so immersed in the wilderness that it is difficult to lead him out. The meaning of day is a cycle of time to be run, that something may be accomplished. Thus, when we read to-day hear my voice, it has taken ages for us to hear the Word of God correct.

We need only to glance over the whole as we view a panorama, and marvel at the scenes as they have been portrayed by our state called infancy, and now recognize even a few who are ready to follow Him, the Way, the Truth and the Light. All of the Bible proves this assertion (when we can see). Galatians v: 19 to 26. Now the works of the flesh are manifest, which are these, adultery, fornication, uncleanness, lasciviousness, idolatry, witchcraft, hatred, variance, emulations, wrath, strife, seditions, heresies, envyings, murders, drunkenness, revellings; and those who are held by the above actions are not to inherit the kingdom of God.

But the fruit of the spirit is love, joy, peace, longsuffering, gentleness, goodness, faith, meekness, temperance; against such there is no law, and they that are Christ's have crucified the flesh with the affections and lusts. If we live in the spirit, let us also walk in the spirit. Let us not be desirous of vain glory, provoking one another, envying one another. If we think ourselves something, when we are nothing, we deceive ourselves. We are to bear each other's burdens, and with God to aid us, we may cast them at His feet.

We trust the very little that has been given as a homeopathy remedy in this little work may awaken an interest in all who will take time to peruse it. It took a long time for us to give old allopathy (creeds and dogmas) a farewell shake, but we found ourselves being left behind, for the car of progress goes rapidly forward with its load of human freight or minds quickened into life and activity through the constant whirl of a busy day, but the night-time comes to every soul, and it is at this time our little book may be picked up with a desire to kill time. We trust that you will not kill the Spirit or the Holy Ghost that calls out

"To-day hear my voice." Like John the Baptist crying in the wilderness we would make ready the way for Him who is to come after, whose shoes we are not worthy to unloose. This is the spirit we have in sending out this "Key," for it will unlock the door to any one of the many mansions that you may be prepared to enter.

When you come into a full understanding of laws and principles, you will sing, I would not live always; I care not to stay. But until you do come into a full understanding you will find it is the storm after storm that develops you, be ready to meet all things, for you can understand why God sends all things to you for your good. Blessings are in the etymology of the Hebrew the same as cursing.

All is from the creative power to unfold your possibilities. Thus you thank God for sending that which draws you nearer unto Him. "I am the vine; ye are the branches." If we do not bear fruit we are to be cut off and cast into the fire. If we do bear fruit we will be operated upon by the angelic ministration and purged that we may bear more fruit. This state pleases the Father. Ephesians 11: 1, 2.

And you hath He quickened who were dead in trespasses and sin, wherein in time past ye walked according to the course of this world, according to the prince of the power of the air, the spirit that now worketh in the children of disobedience.

For by grace are ye saved through faith; and that not of yourselves. It is the gift of God. The whole plan of salvation consists of knowing. Knowledge gives us power, and the gift of God as given to us is knowledge. In the Bible we find the mind is spoken of as the understanding, and we are cautioned with all our getting to get understanding. Simon who answered Jesus was called blessed, because he knew when asked the important question, "Whom do men say that I am?" If it were simply answering the one question that made Simon blessed, we would not recognize in the answer a blessed state, but we find that Simon denotes the understanding, and know the voice that tells Jesus "Thou art Christ, the Son of the living God," is to vibrate in every soul in time, for it is a state of consciousness never to be cut off, against which the gates of hell cannot prevail. It is the Rock of Ages, or Rock of Reason, or the Pearl of Great Price. There are so many ways of expressing the nature when it is understood, and still few understand the nature because it has not been as yet unfolded, but this is the whole plan consummated. To know means to obey the laws as written through ages in the different natures of man.

He who went away has come again; in other

words, Christ has arisen from the dead. We must remember that it has taken all these ages to bring about the state represented by Christ. The work was commenced in Adam or Genesis, when the world was made by God's creative hand in Exodus, the Hebrews marched to gain the promised land, Leviticus contained the law, holy, just and good, Numbers record the tribes enrolled, all sons of Abraham's blood, Moses in Deuteronomy records God's mighty deeds, brave Joshua into Canaan's land the host of Israel leads, in Judges there rebellion oft provokes the Lord to smite, but Ruth records the faith of one well pleased in her sight.

Ruth 1st, 16 verse. And Ruth said, "Entreat me not to leave thee, or to return from following after thee; thy Lord is my God." We find all that has been given in Bible history, all ancient and modern history has been given to man that his mind in time could express itself as Simon of old did: "I know thou art Christ." This is accomplished when the brain structure has been fully developed, and we have the eyes that the Bible speaks of as spiritual; we are able to discern, discriminate, distinguish the difference between intellectual and spiritual things. Rheuben (perception) has been developed to glorify God and God only.

Thus the first faculty must be prepared to do its father's bidding, before we can marshal the other eleven brothers (or faculties), that we may in time present an orderly train of thought which is pleasing to God.

The survival of the fittest in the race for life may be understood when we begin this God-like task of pleasing our Father. The question of who are the fittest we may leave with Him who reads the heart, and as we cast our burdens upon Him, in fact we have no burdens, when we read our title clear, because it is love to God that bears us on and up in the life work set before us. There is no race except as we would put ten thousand inharmonious thoughts to flight, and leave the Ego master of the battle-field. Our work is subjective; we are in the right line to reach the fountain head. We care not for the morrow; to-morrow takes care of itself. The Bible is the grandest book ever written. In time we hope to read it fully from its interior or soul. Swedenborg saw there was a deeper meaning than that implied by the letter. He called it reading between the lines. The power that man in time will inherit will cause him to read aright the Book of Books. This state will be reached through the intellect (Japhet) being developed and resting wholly in the spiritual (Shemitic) nature.

To come in contact with the Lord of Lords or King of Kings requires a nature as is given by Jesus the Christ, and it is to this end that we should know all things. Jesus was given; He came to save us; He died that we might live; and yet we are told that the Messiah is to come again. This we know to be a truth; but we also know, not as before in One Individual, The Messiah, The Anointed One, is He who has been prepared to do His Father's Will, He who comes from a lowly state born in the manger, and lives a life of sacrifice. He who pleases God, and in time receives the just reward, joined or united to his Father, through obedience to His laws and precepts. In spirit we are one with God. God the Father (the creative center or life), God the Son (emanating from the Father), and God the Holy Ghost (the Divine Spirit or breath, the air we are sustained by). His agent, for the spirit draws its life from the soul or center of creation's God.

We must think in the Shemitic line to evolve or unfold the spiritual nature. We know thought moves the world, but we do not send out the right thoughts toward the Creator, or we would show a higher state or nature. The poor millionaire does not know God. His god is in the earth, and he cannot be made to see that he is poor, because he has not a state in his nature for spiritual things. We should pity not blame the poor blind millionaire.

(The millennium means the thousand years of

Christ's reign upon the earth.) We know full well if the Spirit of Christ could be embodied in humanity, that the millennium would be now, and therefore we are millennarians, for we believe this state must come to the fittest who will survive in the race for life.

God gave us the earth and the fullness thereof, but man's nature being perverse by his soul coming in contact with the animal nature, it has caused him to act and to do as we see him from the earliest stage of growth in Adam up to the present day. God saw that we would need a mediator between earth and heaven (the lowest and highest states), and He prepared One, Jesus, (which means to save, to make whole, one in whom all the faculties are developed). Consequently He knew His Father, and His Father knew Him. We have the same privilege, or else God would not have sent His Son to lead us unto Him.

Look well to your thoughts. The meaning of thought is to number, to reckon, compute. Thus we may in time regulate our minds if we watch and pray to do His Will. To know God we must think rightly. To think right is to do right; and to do right pleases Him who watches over us and numbers the hairs of our head.

The River of Water of Life we will then drink and be nourished by as He ordained from the beginning, for he said, "Let there be Light."

The mind must be prepared to do the work as in Adam, (to reason, to think, to compare, to liken, to form similitudes.) We begin in Adam, for the earth must be tilled, cultivated and made ready for the Tree of Life. The garden of Eden is hedged in that fruit may be raised. The mind must be hedged in from the world, as it is in the state called Babylon (relating to spiritual things,) signs and forms, parables and allegories hold the minds of those who are not capable of understanding God. The most unfolded minds are in a chaotic state, for they reason from the intellect, and cannot see with spiritual eyes, because the Shemitic nature has not been developed. We hope you will consider this epistle as sent to you, and call upon God to enlighten you. If, like Paul, we have offended, we trust as did he, for it is with a godly fear we write. If God be with us, who can be against us? It is God that justifieth.

Then give unto Cæsar the things which are Cæsar's but unto God the things which belong to Him, for He is jealous and watches with love and tenderness lest we be cast into the bottomless pit, (ignorance or darkness).

We must be willing to sacrifice those things that hold or bind us to the earth. In the Hebrew sacrifice signifies, in the order in which it is made, processes of soul growth that were to be perfectly made known in the life of Christ, and ultimately in all humanity. As Abraham, was willing to sacrifice Isaac, it brought his soul into a higher state, for faith was established, so may we be brought up by the gradual death of the ruling animal nature, by the transmuting action of fires of affliction and tribulation, by the gift of God in overshadowing the soul, inserting in it germs of life and giving to it laws and precepts of a higher nature.

Paul acknowledged to King Agrippa that he lived after the most or straightest sect of his religion, a Pharisee, and while living the life he thought he ought to do many things contrary to the name of Jesus of Nazareth. He tells the king that he shut up many of the saints in prison, he got mad, blasphemed and persecuted in every synagogue, but on his way to Damascus at midday he saw a light from heaven, above the brightness of the sun. It shone about him and on those who were with him. They all fell to the earth and Paul heard a voice in the Hebrew tongue say, Saul, Saul, (Saul is the same as Paul) why persecutest thou me? Paul answered and said, Who art thou, Lord? And he said, I am Jesus whom thou persecutest; arise, stand upon thy feet; for I have appeared unto thee for this purpose: To make thee a minister and a witness both of these things which thou hast seen, and of those things in which I will appear unto thee, delivering thee from the people, and from the Gentiles, unto whom now I send thee, to open their eyes and to turn them from darkness to light, and from the power of Satan unto God. The Acts xxvi: 5 to 15.

Pharisee means dissimulation, and the meaning of dissimulation is hypocrisy; therefore, we find Paul not in the right path although joined to the straightest sect of religion. The meaning of Paul is a state asking or desiring (born of the tribe of Benjamin). He possessed conscientiousness and desired to please God. He almost persuaded King Agrippa to be a Christian, and Paul said, would to God not only thou, but all that hear me would become as I have been convinced that all the work has been to bring us into a state of knowing. The Jews expected Paul to fall down dead because a viper took hold of his hand when he gathered some wood for a fire; his hand was not even swollen; he was not harmed; then the Jews called him a god.

The meaning of viper or serpent is hissing muttering, that which never goes straight. It resists Truth, Right and Justice on which God insists, therefore, the viper could not stay upon his hand for Paul desired to please God.

In Paul's time we find they were, as in this day. Some believed the things which were spoken, and some believed not. Thus they scattered or departed when they could not agree among them, selves. (The Acts xxviii: 24.) If we desire to know how far we have advanced in relation to spiritual things, let us question how much we know concerning God. We may be, like King Agrippa, almost persuaded to be a Christian, but we must know to be a Christian we should live the life. It is not alone belonging to the straightest sect for we may be Pharisees also.

There is a way out of the wilderness or else there would not have been a wilderness for God does not oppress. It is man's perverse nature that is oppressive.

We, like Paul, must see the light in the heavens and hear the voice, before we know that we are persecuting Jesus.

We know heaven is a perfect state of the mind and the light that Paul saw was in his mind and Reason called out, Why Saul dost thou persecute me? When he was convinced it was Jesus he stood upon his feet, which means a foundation, permanent advancement, progression.

When we hear the voice we will stand firm for the foundation is truth. The understanding has been opened, "We know thou art Christ." But the garden must be hedged in. The silent working of the power of God will bring all the lower nature under control, that the temple, the mind, may be established. Then as you contemplate the workings of His divine laws, your soul rejoices as did Paul and you would like to convert all to the truth. When the lamb and the lion lay down side by side, the millennium has come, for these natures harmonize. Paul denotes a state of soul growth which asks or desires spiritual things.

The Key to the Kingdom may help you to enter. The way is open and you are here invited to join us as Paul invited King Agrippa, and all who heard him that day. Paul told Festus (when he was accused of being mad) that these things were not done in a corner, or hidden from us if we have the desire to seek or knock at the door.

Much learning does not make us mad when the thoughts are directed to God through the Shemitic nature. We know people go mad who are called religious and Paul acknowledged himself to be mad, when in the straightest sect of religion, but the light that came to Paul on his journey revealed all things and he had much learning. He was a servant of Jesus Christ. Paul tells us that the wrath of God is revealed from heaven against all ungodliness and unrighteousness of men, who hold the truth in unrighteousness, for man does not give to God the praise. Man is not thankful to God; he becomes vain and his soul is accordingly obscured; he professes himself to be wise when he is a fool; he changes the glory of the incorruptible God into an image made like to corruptible man. Man has changed the truth of God into a lie, and worshipped and served the creature more than the Creator, who is blessed forever.

God causes the ungodly to be punished. We are now moving toward the truth with rapidity, our intellects are being developed but we are also in a restless state because there is none that understandeth, there is none that seeketh after God. They are all gone out of the way, they are together become unprofitable; there is none that doeth good, no not one. (Rom. iii: 11.) It is time we were awakened to a realization of our situation and put on the armour of faith, putting our houses in order with our lamps trimmed and brightly burning. There are many in our midst whom Jude describes as speaking great swelling words, who admire men's persons because of advantage. But we are cautioned in these last times who should be mockers and walk after their own ungodly lusts.

The sensual have not the Spirit of God in them. It is only God our Saviour who can keep us from falling and bring us into His glory, where we shall be filled with exceeding joy. I am the beginning (Alpha), and the ending (Omega), which is, and which was, and which is to come. This voice or spirit was heard by John on the Isle of Patmos and when he turned to see the voice that spake to him, he saw as we read in Revelations that which caused him great fear and he fell as dead. But the right hand was laid upon John.

The meaning of hand is the same as memory, (to grasp, to hold, to fashion and hew, to yield power, an agency strongly exerted, to guide, to direct, to be firm to go forward, advancement). We find this to be the office of Gad (memory). One of the faculties, John, remembered when the right hand was laid upon him. John was told to write the things that he had seen, for they should come to pass hereafter.

The meaning of seven is (fulfilling a covenant bound by an oath). We are to come into this covenant that He has made with us. His laws are to be fulfilled, and the seven stars are to be unfolded in the mind (the candlesticks represent the faculties.) We are to give forth light; the words would burn as a furnace if we suppressed them. Hide not your light under a bushel, but put it in a candlestick that it may give light unto all who are in the house.

The two-edged sword is the same as in Eden, to protect the Tree of Life. The meaning of sword (lays waste, and would seem to work harm, to cut, to fashion, to form, to hew). These meanings are given to us in the Hebrew etymology, and it is through this channel that we have been led to the soul of the Bible, but it is concealed from us until we put forth as did Saul of old, the cry, "O God, what shall I do to be saved?" The prayer will be answered; for God helps all those who help themselves. We are told the devil will cast some of us into prison that we may be tried, but if we are faithful unto death we will receive the crown of life.

"He that hath an ear let him hear what the Spirit saith unto the churches." Rev. 11: 29.

"He that overcometh shall not be hurt of the second death."

To him that overcometh will I give to eat of the hidden manna. Rev. 11: 17.

To him who overcometh and keepeth my works unto the end, to him will I give power over the nations. Rev. 11: 26.

I come quickly and my reward is with me, to every man according as his works shall be.

He that testifieth these things saith, Surely I come quickly. Amen.

"Amen" is the Hebrew word for "faith," which it defines as the union of the mind of man with God through knowledge of law and obedience thereto.

We would not take up this work of His unless somewhat prepared to enter into the interior or soul of things. We do not profess to know much more than the first letter of the alphabet. But from Aleph we took our first lesson.

Every man is brutish in his knowledge: every founder is confounded by the graven image: for his molten image is falsehood, and there is no breath in them: for the pastors have become brutish and have not sought the Lord: therefore they shall not prosper, and all their flocks shall be scattered. Jer. x: 14 to 21.

In our work we must know of the first and the last. Simon (the understanding) serves us as the foundation or rock that our church may rest upon; if the winds blow and the storms beat against this foundation it remains firm or sure.

The people who were in the valley while Moses was on the mount writing the Laws remained longer than a few days. The meaning of day (in the etymology of the Hebrew) is a time set apart to perform a certain work, a full cycle, that the work may be completed. We read in Genesis the world was created in six days, but know it took ages. Some good people will not question or try to find out for themselves what the Bible really does mean, but take it for granted that God (whom they do not know) is all powerful. They say if the Bible was written by God it satisfies them, for they cannot doubt Him (whom they know not of); if the Bible reads six days, of course they (dear souls) believe it. (Ignorance in this case is bliss), but we do not think it folly to be wise, for the Bible reiterates again and again that wisdom is the principal thing to get hold of. "With all thy getting get understanding." Prov. iv: 7.

So it is we start out on our mission, having only learned the first letter in the Hebrew (Aleph), which denotes in its primary sense the subdued nature of the animal. The letter was drawn from the face of an ox. We cannot advance in spiritual things until the animal in our nature is subdued; and Jesus personified this statement. Paul tells us we worship an unknown God, and we cannot deny his statement until we know what the true God is. The soul of the Bible was purposely concealed from us, in other words, we were not ready to read the Bible aright before now. In this we see the wisdom of God. The outer meaning of the Bible proves, as the statement given by Paul, we are worshipping ignorantly; but Paul got the light, and he knew the truth; therefore Paul was not afraid to tell it, even to King Agrippa.

It does not require one to wear long, flowing garments, or to imitate the look in the oxen's face. Neither will give you the light Paul saw; and it is this light that God speaks of as coming to every soul that is in darkness. Your Free Will, combined with Understanding, (Asher and Simon, faculties of the mind) will take you into the pleasant pastures and beside the still waters that

David enjoyed, because God loved David, the God that loved Paul.

Paul planted, and Appolos watered; it was for God to give the increase. So with our work, we do our part, and leave the rest with Him who reads the heart.

In parting with the "Key," let us represent it as worthy of consideration. St. Peter has been (and now is to some) a symbol, the predecessor or outward of the coming power, but when we like Peter, are received into fellowship with Jesus, and receive the new name, Cephas—a stone, because he was firm and unyielding in righteousness, a rock, the human understanding, then we enjoy the fellowship as given by Jesus, for it opens the understanding, and we cannot deny our Master.

Although there may be Herods who cannot favor us, we know their house is left to them desolate, and they cannot see Jesus until the time comes when they shall say, "Blessed is He that cometh in the name of the Lord." We take the same ground that Jesus did when asked "Is it lawful to heal on the Sabbath Day?" We do our work as then; when duty calls us we are ready.

Again we take the position of the poor woman who desired to fulfil in the largest measure her obligation to God. We cast in our mite and desire no eye but His to fall upon it. Our contribution is small. But we know "The hour has come when the Son of Man should be glorified."

"If any man serve me, let him follow me; and where I am there shall also my servant be; if any man serve me, him will my Father honor."

"Walk while ye have the light, lest darkness overtake you; be the children of light."

If we were not in the state called darkness there would not have been so much said about the light. It is the light that was first sent, but the darkness comprehended it not. Now we are trying to assist the darkened mind that the truth may flash in upon it as with Paul when on his journey, he was crucifying Jesus, the Light of Reason illuminated his mind, he saw his error and asked God to forgive him. Let us be true to our highest state; if convinced that we are in the dark, seek diligently for the pure gold thrice proven. Ask what you will in my name; that will I give unto you. Where is the church that can save your soul? It is a means unto an end, but it is not the end. I am Alpha and Omega, the beginning and the end. Give God all the praise, all the honor, all the glory, and you are His Son, then your mind like His dearly beloved can read all things. You are one with God.

Our principal object in sending this "Key" forward is that all of God's children may be enlightened and blest through spiritual knowledge.

We would assist each of His children to enter the kingdom if it were possible. The way is now open, and if you have the desire to know God or the truth, you will be set free, as the writer of this little work is each day made to realize more fully the wonderful workings of the creative power of God. This state goes on when we direct our thoughts into the highest channel (the spiritual), and His words made manifest, "I send my Son to save the world."

Jesus has come to the mind that can conceive Jesus as a pure life; we must Live It. The kingdom is then established upon the earth; it has always been in heaven. Heaven is an expanse, something beaten out, broadened, made to hold. Thus the mind is through the intellectual nature unfolded and dwelling upon spiritual things Japhet rests in time in the tents of Shem. Gen. ii: 5.

The mind is led from signs and forms to the truth through the etymology of the Hebrew and Greek, as given by Ghesenious, Parkhurst and others. God's orderly method in creation is then made clear to the eye that can see, and you enter unto the kingdom.

Unto Shem also, the father of all the children of Eber, (the meaning of Eber is crossing the river) the brother of Japhet the elder, even to him were children born. Gen. x: 21.

Water in all its form indicates creative power,

energy or motion (in the etymology of the Hebrew). Then we read that Eber's children crossed the swift, flowing river in the Jordan (overcoming their low nature thereby), or they were instructed in spiritual things and delivered by Joshua, whose name means the same as Jesus. Joshua saved the children of Israel, who are to forever praise Jehovah for the great wealth bestowed upon them, possessing blessings of wisdom and health.

To be a son of God and heir to the eternal kingdom, we must be the children of Shem (or spirituality); then all confusion is banished from the mind, the wilderness is passed, and the manna from heaven sustains us. This is God's promise. Gen. ix: 27.

This is the covenant, saith the Lord, if ye keep my commandments, I will be to you a God, and ye shall be my people. Ask what ye will in my name, that will I give unto you.

Let us ask for more light or reason, which God declared in the beginning was, but the darkness could not comprehend it. Adam and Eve were naked, but were not ashamed. Gen. ii: 25. Why? Because they could not reason; their minds were very low or feeble. This state was naked or unadorned.

We are now beginning to reason, as we have partially cultivated the garden, and Adam, the earth, gives us this product, reason. It is the light of the Logos, word or speak that was at the beginning; it was God and is God. Now we see, our eyes are open; we understand and perceive our nakedness.*

Banah (house) means the same as Son (in the etymology of the Hebrew). The temple or house mind is not yet complete; thus reason cannot be sent forth. That this is the rock or stone that was laid at the mouth of the den, which the king sealed with his signet, there can be no doubt, for Dan denotes judgment, and the lions did not hurt Daniel, because God said, Fear not Daniel, for from the first day that thou didst set thine heart to understand and to chasten thyself before thy God, thy words were heard. The angel said, O, man greatly beloved, fear not, peace be unto thee, stand upright and fear not, Daniel. Thus he overcame the lions in the den. Because he had faith in God he was to be steadfast forever, and his kingdom is not to be destroyed; he is to have dominion unto the end. This is what (Dan) judgment will do for us, when we like Daniel set our hearts to understanding God. This state worketh wonders in the earth, for men tremble and fear before the God of Daniel. He is the living God.

---

*Thus, if the low state should peep and mutter as wizzards, we know their eyes are not yet open, they cannot discern good from evil, right from wrong.

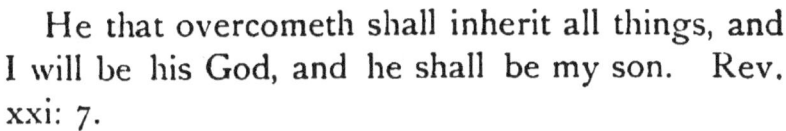

He that overcometh shall inherit all things, and I will be his God, and he shall be my son. Rev. xxi: 7.

This passage does not give us reason to think that sin (ignorance) is to be overcome or pardoned by the prayers of another. There can be no doubt that ignorance in time will be overcome.

Our salvation is assured when we know God. Then in this glorious age of reason why not ask for more light concerning spiritual things. All things are promised to those who overcome ignorance.

We reiterate the Bible is the travail of the soul, or the history of the human family, as it began in Adam and was perfected in Jesus the Christ.

Then let us admire wisdom, even in the little ant, who is wise and prepares its meat in the summer. Prov. xxx: 25.

Being born again, not of corruptible seed, but of incorruptible, by the word of God, which liveth and abideth forever. Peter i: 23.

Let us ascend once more together on the mount with our twelve principal faculties developed to praise God. We like Paul understand (through our ignorance) we worshipped the unknown God.

We were thereby held in the signs and forms, by parables and allegories, isms and creeds, but we now see, know and understand that they were all as necessary in the unfoldment of the mind as the various means or grades are offered to the child until it can reason for itself.

Reason is God. This is our rock, and eternal is its foundation. The soul of the Bible has given us the truth. The husk was necessary, for we have been in the low or swine state, but now we desire to be sons of God and heirs to the Eternal Kingdom; therefore we are called to partake of the hidden manna, the Bread of Life, that which sustains the soul.

To eat of the Tree of Knowledge we must obey His Will in all things. Exodus 23. The angel that He has sent to bring us into the place which He has prepared, we must obey. We are not to provoke him, for he will not pardon our transgressions. God's name is in this angel. We are told if we obey the angel's voice and do all that God speaks, then our enemies and adversaries are to be overcome by God. This angel is to cut off forever the Amorites, and the Hitties, the Perizzites, and the Canaanites, the Hivites, and the Jebusities; these are our enemies (our evil or wrong thoughts, desires, appetites and propensities). They are to be utterly overthrown, and their images broken down. Then we may worship the Lord our God for he blesses our bread and water. He takes away sickness from our midst. He tells us this work is to be done little by little not in one year, (well we know this to be a truth), lest the land become desolate, and the beasts of the field multiply against our higher nature before it is fully established. God will put these tribes to flight just as He does all of His work gradually; then the angel leads us to the fountain head, for we no longer wander in confusion. Simon (the understanding) is developed, and "we know it is Christ." This is the sum and substance of our life, to acquire knowledge, and with all our getting we are told to get understanding. To reconstruct or rearrange the material that we have now at hand will keep us for a time busy; regeneration or a new birth cannot come to the individual mind until it is through with signs and forms as we find them to-day in the churches. We must know God in truth, the high and mighty God who numbered the heavens, and ordered the earth, who created all things for a wise purpose, who made man in the image and likeness of Himself, (how far are we now from the Perfected One?). The mind of man was to be gradually built, then it calls out to know God and finds the true temple, then develop perception (Rheuben) to see. It was from the beginning ordained that we should be led just as we have been until we know through perception (our first faculty) that the true temple (the mind) was built without the sound of a hammer. All things are made clear to the eye that can see and the ear that hears. The cold-hearted selfishness must be overcome by love to God and man. We are one family; He is our Father; the brotherhood is bound by Christ who gave His life to save ours from ignorance, which is sin and death. Let us on our journey heavenward do as Jesus did, call all men brothers. He said to those who told Him that His mother and sisters were waiting outside the temple for Him, It was those who did the Will of His Father who were His sisters and His mother. Can we not draw near to God in this same spirit of truth, and do His Will then in return we know all things for Simon is unfolded within us, and our visit to the mount will always give us strength, because we reason with the twelve (not one or two faculties).

The state of consciousness that Jesus possessed we may also enjoy, when we like Him are willing to do our Father's bidding. Jesus came to fulfil the Law, not to destroy it. He brought us grace and truth. When the understanding (Simon) is developed you will see all things as they are; God directs us in the highest channel when we obey His voice, which comes from the interior or Ark of the Covenant. John makes ready the way for Him who is mightier, as John baptizes with water, but Christ baptizes with the Holy Ghost; let us get out of the wilderness in this enlightened age and not grope about in the dark, following strange or false Gods, provoking the true and living God with our ignorance. Our philosophy or science is not new (but as old as the world;) it was laid with the foundation of the world; it is the Logos or Word that was at the beginning; it is reason the same that was thrown in upon Paul's mind as he was on his way to Damascus; it outshone the brightness of the sun; he was told to stand upon his feet and go forth as a minister to turn all with whom he came in contact from darkness to light, and from the power of Satan to God, that they might receive forgiveness of sins. This is what our New (or old) Philosophy will do for those who are ready to turn from the creeds and dogmas of the present day that hold the mind in darkness. We must reason and think for ourselves that we like Paul may obey the voice of Jesus. Light will rule prejudice or darkness out of existence; follow Him and Him only if you would be truly happy.

The inner meaning of the Bible tells us the Garden of Eden stands for the physical system controlled by the soul of man; all that is related of it must describe different parts and functions of the human body.

Thus the river of Eden stands for the stream of vital power, nervous energy, which governs the performance of the organic functions of the body.

This river has its rise in the nerve centers of the brain, and from thence it is parted and becomes into four heads; that is, it distributes power to the four fundamental departments of the animal economy. Circulation is represented in the Bible, Gen. ii, as the river Pison and called the first river, compassing the whole land of Havilah Respiration, is represented by Gihon the second river mentioned in Genesis as that which compasseth the whole land of Ethiopia. Digestion is represented as the third river Hiddekel, which goeth toward the East of Assyria; the fourth river is Generation and in the Bible is called Euphrates, (L. of L.) We would not here refer to these rivers except to prove our assertion that man as yet knows nothing of himself (subjectively), consequently can not know God. As the infant possesses innately the attributes of manhood and yet cannot make them known till after many years. So it is with man; from his primitive state it has taken a process of growth and extention to bring the mind where it may stand alone with God. We have been so feeble in the race that we have not understood law; how then could we conform to it? We have blindly worshipped water, fire, trees, mountains and men, but now we must develop our understanding and say as did Simon of old, "I know thou art the Christ." This state gives us peace, joy and everlasting pleasure. This state pleases God and He blesses us for striving to learn of Him through His works and ways in Creation; then science will shake hands with religion and all men are brothers because we could not believe like Thomas, until we put our hand in the hole in His side. It caused hard feelings to exist as Paul stated to King Aggrippa. We were thrust into prison and left to starve as we could not see or think like those who essayed to be Christians, for they belonged to the strictest sect as did Paul, until his eyes were opened by the light of Reason.

All men will be as brothers in time, but the change will come gradually as each soul feels the fire of affliction; it melts or softens the cold heartedness toward our fellow men; we must look upon ourselves as souls sent here to do a work to become Sons of God and heirs to the kingdom of heaven; then we extend the right hand of fellowship.

If the prayer from each soul can go forth to God for light and is sent from the interior or Ark of the Covenant, (no formulated prayer for the unfolded mind) then the light will come and we will be Pauls seeking to draw all men to God. No house of worship is needed by Paul he worshipped in spirit and truth. It would be well if we could take some of our costly edifices reared skyward and built for the exterior worship of God, as was inscribed on the altar in Athens, To the Unknown. It would be well we say, to turn the same into free homes, educate the poor, feed the poor, then you may lead the poor to God; scatter the gold, God gave it freely; the bread of Life is of much more value and this you receive in return. Jesus said, "The poor ye have always with you. We should understand that he meant the nature of man was yet so low or poor that we always have an opportunity to do better, this state Jesus loved because He brought it up higher each time He expressed His nature. Then let Jesus speak in all our actions and the poor we will befriend. God is the Father of both rich and poor. If we are covetous the sin will fall upon our heads. Vengeance is mine, saith the Lord.

We should be ready to enter the promised land our rightful inheritance. God's gift to man, a mind at rest because it knows God and is happy. Love to God will cause us to extend our hand to the neighbor and assist all souls to the highest state in existence, which is to know our Father, through obedience to His Will we enter the Kingdom of Heaven for a Son of God and heir to the highest kingdom, will represent Immanuel, God in the flesh. The entire process of regeneration consists of refusing evil and choosing good as a principle of life.

This work can be better performed when we understand God's plan for our redemption. It must be admitted that there is more pleasure in possessions acquired through individual exertion to obtain the same, than if we have possessions bestowed upon us gratuitously. Thus the law of compensation holds good in all departments of our lives, but more especially in the Spiritual is it understood. We know it is more blessed to give than to receive, for the giving constitutes a law and the blessing is sure to follow.

The Bible was created to lead man from his infant state in Adam, up to the perfect state Jesus the Christ.

We claim no one can worship God as they should (which is to overcome ignorance), to have fixed and stamped upon the mind the orderly process by which all life has come forth from that eternal creative cause made known in the names of Elohim and Jehovah. It is to know the way by which the life of God has gone forth, entered into and become a part of everything that has existence. It is to understand and obey the laws He has written through ages of development in the physical, intellectual and moral natures of man. This prepares the way for a knowledge of Christ, which principle must be embodied in our lives to have power from the Most High, (L. of L.)

The iniquity or ignorance of the parent shall

descend to the children from generation to generation, whereas, if the parents have overcome their ignorance by a life guided and governed by the Anointed One, as love to their fellowman, etc., then health, virtue and goodness are transmitted to the offspring. In time the low, selfish nature will be overcome by the highest, which is God.

"Let us give to Cæsar those things which belong to Cæsar, but unto God the things that belong to God."

It has required these long years (1800) to build the mind of man (God's greatest work), where it may now unflinchingly speak the truth as God ordained it should in time know the truth and free itself. We have as religionists, 1st, Jews, 7,931,080; 2nd, Christians, 380,000,000; 3rd, Mohammedans, 200,000,000; 4th, Brahmins, 177,000,000; 5th, Buddhists, etc., 450,000,000, according to statistical writers is the present religious population of the globe. Then this population is divided into twenty or more denominations, proving conclusively man is not yet able to see face to face or he would be worshipping from the temple built without the sound of a hammer; then all would see alike from the true temple. 11 Chron. 2. The building of this temple has taken all these years, when now a few, a very few, from out of the many religionists are prepared to read the Book of Books understandingly. If we are ready to take up the cross and follow Him who is the way, the truth and the light, then we enter the city of Jerusalem. Solomon means peaceful. This state leads us; our work is subjective, and we must read aright the Word of God to worship in truth.

This state can only be reached when we have outgrown or have no further use for any of the religions that man has established upon the earth. All things have been necessary, but progression is God's law, and we advance to make use of our free or individual Will, guided by His Will who tells us to come unto Him for the true rest our soul craves; we find it, and bow to our loving Father's Will for establishing our minds as like Solomon we also ask God for wisdom and knowledge above all else, and our prayer is answered; we now understand something of the mind of man.

"Man lived upon this planet and delved into the earth before he was able to read the record written in the rocks by the finger of the Almighty, telling of the gradual processes employed, and the immense periods of time required in its formation. It no longer seems incredible, as otherwise it might, that learned theologians and philologists should have critically analyzed and compared every word and letter in the original Scriptures, and yet never caught a glimpse of the real significance of those root etymologies which in the Law of Laws are shown to reveal the same orderly method of creation in the domain of Mind that Geology unfolds in the realm of matter. The heavens have been searched and the component forces and factors of earth and air and sea, closely investigated and carefully classified, disclosing the many and mighty fixed principles operating through nature in all its forms.

For the performance of this work, grand and necessary as it has been, intellectual perception is all that has been required; but for the discovery and apprehension of the Law of Laws, a spiritual perception is essential. All things are made clear through a study of these works. The origin of man and his evolution, the reason of the differences of races, languages and religions, the true nature of the new birth and redemption, the condition of the disembodied soul, heaven, hell and probation after death are presented so that the method of God in the progressive creation of man is as easily understood as the first principles of science. All the labor and striving of men and nations in the past, as portrayed in every department of human history, are shown as an outwrought expression of the inworking of the Divine Power, preparing the foundation, broad and strong, in the physical, intellectual and moral natures of man for the glorious superstructure, the spiritual, which brings Christ universal into the souls of men." (Quotation from Law of Laws.)

We must free ourselves from all doctrines to adore the true and living God in nature. God reads the heart; He knows His sheep and we know our shepherd; therefore we do not swell the number as Religionists. We cultivate the spiritual garden (the mind) and destroy the tares and thistles least they choke out the Word of God (which means to number or order all things according to grade.) God is Law and we must live by law to please the Maker of Laws. The soul of the Bible was purposely concealed until now, when some minds are strong enough to demand the meat or food prepared and found in the etymology of the Hebrew—all we require to open our spiritual eyes. We then receive and are born from above (the head) or the Mind is unfolded and we see all things clear, not trough the glass darkly. This is Simon Peter, the Understanding, the Key to the Kingdom of Heaven a state of consciousness which we enter into while living on earth.

These books for sale at news dealers or 942 Valencia St., S. F.

It seemed good to me also, having had perfect understanding of all things from the very first, to write unto thee in order, most excellent Theophilus (one who loves God), that thou mightest know the certainty of those things, wherein thou hast been instructed. St. Luke 1: 3, 4.

W. M. R. DIMOND.

FROM OBJECTIVE TO SUBJECTIVE.

We find in our study that Jacob's twelve sons
Went off as the tribes, thus history runs.
As twelve tribes of Israel they go to explore
The land and the sea; but now we implore
The mind that is ready to reason and think,
To turn their thoughts into the garden, this link
As in Eden, we cannot deny, faculties are broadened
If with God we abide; we reason and think
As never before, for all is made clear if the mind will explore.
We would not prevaricate, why should we try?
We now know the reason, the where and the why,
For God does enlighten the mind, if 'twill turn
From the signs, forms and symbols, if willing to learn
Of His orderly method, as seen in creation
Where all is made clear, and with due admiration
We behold God in all things; we now find the truth,
All that is established, and all have a worth,
From the least to the greatest, from man unto God.
The mind now unfolds; by His blessed mode
We are slowly prepared to reason and think
For ourselves; then we find the long missing link
Through churches established. They all do their work
For those who require them; we will not shirk
The way God has opened; we follow His plan.
It leads to salvation, and man unto man
Cannot give this great gift; it is God's.
When you seek, you shall find.
This we know through His Word, and thus speak our mind.

THE TWELVE PRINCIPAL FACULTIES OF THE MIND.

Rheuben is perception, to see or to know,
Simon, understanding, in truth it is so;
Levi, association, this faculty links,
Judah, with Abraham, faith it represents;
Dan stands for judgment, to choose, to decide,
Napthali, crafty, let it not abide;
Gad, which is memory, labors to pierce,
Asher, the will, let its firmness ne'er cease;
Issiacher is selfish, let it be denied,
Zebelum is social, have pleasure, not pride;
Joseph, constructive, is laden with thought,
Benjamin, conscientious, the spirit has wrought.

LET THERE BE LIGHT.

Let us throw forth these twelve great lights;
They will illumine the mind; our nights
Would be both dark and drear,
If 'twere not for constellations though faculties here;
For we have turned to look within
And find the truth; we know that sin
Is that which changes, can't endure;
Which truth opposes, and will secure
In time, as ignorance is evil too,
And perishes, but this we know,
That God created Man or Mind
To be spiritualized, though still we're blind.

THE FIRST FRUITS.

As each soul unfolds like a flower,
  And turns unto God with a prayer,
'Twill know the true God from that hour;
  Creeds, signs and forms then disappear.

Let us stand firm and fast by our Maker,
    The God of our soul, which is He
Who's awakened; it slept as a creature,
    But now we sing praises to Thee.

Then direct your thoughts to the Godhead;
    Seek early and late till you find
Your Saviour within, for in your head
    Is the soul; it's imprisoned by mind.

God gave it to you, then return it;
    The Father was pleased with but One.
It was Jesus, the Christ, and He teacheth
    The love of His Father as Son.

God sent His dear Son as a pattern
    Or type; shall we follow His plan?
Then kill God's opponent, old Satan,
    For this is the work given man.

We find that our earthy is Adam,
    Its opposite known to be Eve;
The garden of Eden with culture
    Brings forth divine product as seed.

The seed that was thrown by the wayside
    It fell on the soil; 'twas prepared
And bore at the harvest an hundred;
    God watched it, and with us He shared.

Oh, let the good seed scatter freely,
    Prepare then the Adam or earth;
Let Eve do her part to receive it,
    When in the new life we have birth.

Except ye are born from above then,
    Which means in the Head, for we know
We cannot commune with our Father
    While dwelling on earth or below.

Then stir up the soil in your nature,
    Let God speak to you from the soul;
Dominion you'll have o'er the creature,
    As written by Him on the scroll.

www.ingramcontent.com/pod-product-compliance
Lightning Source LLC
Chambersburg PA
CBHW020859160426
43192CB00007B/999